MW00846762

MEDIEVAL WRESTLING

MEDIEVAL WRESTLING

MODERN PRACTICE OF A FIFTEENTH CENTURY MARTIAL ART

JESSICA FINLEY

Freelance Academy Press, Inc, Wheaton, IL 60189
www.freelanceacademypress.com

© 2014 Jessica Finley
All rights reserved.

No portion of this book may be reproduced by any process or technique,
without the express written consent of Freelance Academy Press, Inc.

Photography by Derek Taylor
Additional work by Robert N. Charrette
Cover and book design by Robert N. Charrette

Printed in the United States of America
by Publishers' Graphics

21 20 19 18 17 16 14 13 12 1 2 3 4 5

ISBN: 978-1-937439-11-8

Library of Congress Control Number: 2014932139

For

RST

who set me on this path…

For

CHT

who points the way down it…

For

the students

who remind me why I walk it still.

ACKNOWLEDGEMENTS

There are many people whom I must thank for their contributions to this work.

First, I'd like to thank my husband, Frank Finley. You always believed I could write this thing even though I didn't think I had it in me. Thank you for doing the hundred little things that made writing possible logistically, and for the innumerable times you told me I simply had no choice but to finish this project.

To my instructor Christian Tobler, without whose confidence in my ability and the occasional necessary kick in the pants, this work would never have been completed. Thank you for not only pulling me from ahead, but pushing me from behind.

Also to Gregory Mele who has been a constant source of inspiration to me both personally and professionally, thank you. I am so glad to have gotten the chance to know you, to learn from you, and to call you a friend.

To my brothers- and sisters-in-arms of the Selohaar Fechtschule and the Chicago Swordplay Guild, thank you for your cheers from across the country. We will continue to find ways to train together in the future.

I would also like to thank Roger Siggs for his keen advice on instruction and his no-nonsense approach to all things in life.

To Pete Kautz, thank you for your tips on personal achievement in martial arts. As you suggested, I scrawled "Write a book on Ott" in my training manual years ago as one of three long-term goals. All three have now been achieved and replaced with new ones.

To Jörg Bellinghausen, thank you for your help translating strange bits of obscure German texts on ancient sports. You are a wonderful friend, and I hope someday to make you proud by properly pronouncing *Fühlen*.

To Arden Cowherd, thank you for your instruction and unending encouragement to me. You taught me many invaluable lessons, not just about Judo, but about life and myself.

I must thank the Great Plains Fechtschule: David Stone, James Spruengli, Jim Bowen and Sara Matthias and the many other students who have come trained with me over the years. Also thanks belong to Scott Cozad and my students at Old Dominion Fechtschule who have joined me in training in Virginia.

Most special thanks go to Aron Montaini who has acted as throwing dummy, interpretation sounding board, and especially as my friend and co-instructor. Thank you for putting up with so many classes filled with too much Ott and not enough swords during this process.

Lastly, I would like to thank Derek Taylor for shooting the beautiful photographs for this book.

TABLE OF CONTENTS

INTRODUCTION

The first time I read Ott's treatise on wrestling, I found myself immediately mesmerized. It spoke to me in a way that I hadn't yet experienced with a medieval treatise on fighting. I called Christian Tobler, my instructor, and asked if he'd interpreted the work yet and could I have copies of what he'd done with it. He told me that while he'd done some interpretive work; he had nothing written from which I could study. Then he encouraged me to interpret it myself using my experience in both Medieval German Martial Arts and judo to guide me. After many years of work and development of the interpretations, this book was born.

This book is designed to be a student's working guide to studying Ott's treatise. This is a book that you tuck into your gym bag and carry to training sessions. It isn't meant to be the final word on medieval wrestling, but to launch earnest students on their own studies of medieval wrestling. While I have included a brief, "academic" introduction to the work, it is the interpretations which were my focus when writing this book and it is from these interpretations I expect the reader to gain the most benefit.

Composing a scholarly work on any medieval treatise on the fighting arts is incredibly difficult. While many discoveries have been made in this field, there is still much which is simply unknown. Some of the treatises were copied numerous times, indicating their popularity with the intended audience, and yet we know little or nothing about the actual author. Sometimes we have hints from study in other areas of medieval life, such as legal or monastic records of physical encounters. But with as many inroads that have been made, there is still much work to be done.

I have begun with a short explanation of the fighting arts of medieval Germany in order to introduce the reader to the setting in which this art was originally created. It is, however, well beyond the scope of this project to fully explore the topic. For the reader interested in the greater subject of Medieval European Martial Arts there are many other books which expand upon this subject and can be found listed in the bibliography.

I next share the little that is known about Ott the person and some of my speculations about what his job description might have been. I hope that this section provides some enterprising young researcher the inspiration to delve into this realm further. In order to better understand the context of medieval wrestlers, we must know more about the situations in which they wrestled. Were they wrestling in open tournaments or planned matches; for fun, for high stakes, or (as I suspect) both? The answers to these questions are more than academic, as they affect how one interprets the techniques shown. For instance, when we see an arm break or joint lock, are we being told to actually break the arm or dislocate the joint? Or are we being shown a technique which can be used to gain submission from our opponent thereby winning a "friendly" match? I provide my impressions and hope that future research in this area clarifies the truth.

Next is a short technical analysis of Ott's treatise, explaining a little more about the organization of the work and my treatment of it. In this book I use a translation of the copy of Ott's treatise that is contained within the Von Danzig *Fechtbuch*, despite there being numerous other copies of his work. In this I have followed the advice of wrestling scholar Rainer Welle, who refers to the Von Danzig copy as being the *Leithandschrift* or the "Primary Treatise", in his thesis '... *und wisse das alle höbischeit kompt von deme ringen' Der Ringkampf als adelige Kunst im 15. Und 16. Jahrhundert*. The various copies of the treatise are not identical, and while I note differences between von Danzig and other copies as necessary, I make no claims to have provided an exhaustive list of these differences.

I have chosen to restrict my presentation of the "von Danzig" manuscript to an English translation provided by Christian Tobler and initially published in *In St. George's Name: An Anthology of Medieval Martial Arts*. Unless otherwise noted, any quote from the von Danzig manuscript derives from Mr. Tobler's work.

Moving from the realm of academia, we come to the meat of this book, which is the interpretive work on the techniques themselves. Beginning with some general guidelines and instructions for the student who may not have grounding in another wrestling art, I then introduce the two main grips used in Ott's treatise, followed by each technique and its counter, if any, including notes for any possible variations mentioned in Ott's work. Purists should note that I have chosen to present the techniques in a different order from the original treatise, for reasons which are explained in the section Treatment of the Techniques.

Finally, I have concluded the book with a few appendices including Ott's treatise in its original order of presentation, some drills and training advice, and finally a table by Dr. Welle that shows the interconnection of each of the known copies of Ott's treatise.

I have been working with Ott's treatise for nearly seven years and it has been a truly amazing mental and physical journey. During this time my interpretations have been developed, revised, outright changed, thrown out, revisited, and, in some cases, returned to where I began. Interpretation of a medieval *Fechtbuch* is something that is truly an artistic pursuit, in the medieval sense of the word. It bridges the worlds between art and science: requiring the ability to imagine in three dimensions and to think in new ways and also requiring the ability to stay within the basic rules of martiality and to withstand the rigor of peer review. In all martial arts we find both beauty and structure.

I hope that you find this book to be useful in your training and that it helps you to take your study of the medieval martial arts to a deeper level.

-Jessica Finley
Winter 2013

1

Martial Arts of Medieval Germany

When a modern person thinks of medieval battle, they think of knights, armor and swords. The great secret of the Middle Ages is that knights were not only highly-trained martial artists who wielded lance, spear, sword and dagger with grace and skill, but who also trained in unarmed combat: kicking, punching and wrestling.

As with all martial arts, those of medieval Germany (or more properly, the German-speaking portions of the Holy Roman Empire) weren't created in a vacuum, but rather built on generations of previous experience passed down from master to student. Medieval masters-at-arms sought noble patronage, and hoped to secure financial security by training noble sons in the art of war and by providing tactical expertise to their liege. We know the names of some of these masters through their *Fechtbucher* or "fight-books." These *Fechtbucher* recorded specific instructions on martial techniques with a variety of weapons and in a variety of situations, and sometimes even included such esoterica as siege weapons, gunpowder recipes or specialized dueling weapons. Some of these manuscripts appear to have been commissioned by a noble patron, others were written much like a résumé, showcasing the author's experience and prowess, and yet others appear to have been the personal notebooks of the masters themselves.

Even with the great diversity that medieval German fight masters exemplify in their written works, the one thread that holds these martial artists together over nearly three hundred years of martial development is the knightly martial art created by the grandmaster Johannes Liechtenauer. We know little about him personally; however Liechtenauer was recognized as having primacy of place by a long lineage of medieval fight masters. He encrypted his fighting art into approximately 350 lines of rhyming couplets, generally known as the *Merkverse* ("teaching verse") or *Zettel* ("epitome"). This verse seems to have a dual purpose: first to obscure the teachings to the uninitiated and second, to serve as a mnemonic device to allow students to remember the important points of the art.[1] Fortunately, the modern practitioner was left with not only the verses, which are often frustrating in their obscurity, but also the glosses of the later masters such as Hans Talhoffer, Paulus Kal and Peter Falkner who expanded on the verse, adding their own instruction to Liechtenauer's.

The martial system of Johannes Liechtenauer encompasses the personal combat skills for fighting with the two-handed longsword without armor (*Bloßfechten*), for fighting on horseback (*Roßfechten*), and finally for fighting in armor on foot (*Harnischfechten*). It is through this core longsword curriculum that Master Liechtenauer appears to instruct his students, and through them the knightly class of Germany, on the principles of his *Kunst des Fechten* ("Art of Fighting"). He introduces a conceptual framework that, once one has studied the longsword, can be applied to all other weapons in the art form, even if they aren't directly referenced within the *Zettel*. Later German masters used the *Zettel* to apply in new and sometimes surprising ways to other weapons such as the *messer*, a long, curved, single-handed knife and to the *rappir*, a slender, sharply-pointed weapon used primarily for dueling.

While nearly all of the *Fechtbucher* contain the *Zettel* and one or more master's gloss on Liechtenauer's verse, quite often these books were actually compendiums of small treatises. They could contain a wide variety of masters' treatises on different weapons and topics. These compendiums may have been "made to order" for a particular noble who would request particular masters' works, or they could have been compiled somewhat at random by a scribe who was simply instructed to create a compendium of fighting treatises without specific direction as to which treatises to copy. Either way, the result is that we have a variety of different *Fechtbucher* within which we can find a single treatise copied multiple times across a variety of books.

---

[1] Tobler, Christian. *Fighting with the German Longsword*, p. 2.

2

MASTER OTT, THE BAPTISED JEW

While there are many wrestling techniques contained within numerous medieval treatises, arguably no single person was more influential to medieval wrestling in Germany than the "wrestling master to the princes of Austria":[2] Ott the "baptized Jew."[3] His techniques were copied to no less than 10 separate medieval and renaissance manuscripts spanning nearly 200 years.

We have no idea when Master Ott was born, but he was likely deceased by 1452, the date of the "Von Danzig" manuscript (Codex 44 A 8), where he is given the memorial dedication "God have mercy on him". Ott is listed in the manuscript of Paulus Kal, likely composed in the 1470s, as having been a wrestling master to the princes of Austria and one of the masters of the society of Johannes Liechtenauer, all of whom appear to be deceased at that time. The earliest work attributed to him, the 1443 Talhoffer Manuscript (MS Chart. A 558, Gotha) lacks this memorial blessing, which makes it enticing to conclude that at that time he was still alive, but this supposition also has some problems if one considers the negative attitude towards Jews in Austria and persecution by the Austrian Dukes in the years around 1443.

---

[2] Von Danzig.

[3] "Baptized Jew" literally meaning that he had converted to Christianity.

There are two modern secondary sources which reference Ott and seem to be filled with tantalizing but likely erroneous tidbits of information:

> 1971 Encyclopaedia Judaica says "In 1443 there was a registration of a Jew who knew 'wrestling without shedding blood'. In the 16th century there was a famous Austrian Jew by the name of Ott who was outstanding at the Augsburg games and was even invited to the court of the Austrian prince in order to train the courtiers. He wrote a book in which wrestling was separated from fencing for the first time and was known as 'Ottish Wrestling'."[4]

> Freehof (1965) says, "The first Jewish world champion in any sport was produced in the middle ages. Ott, a converted Jew, who was athletic adviser to Frederick III, emperor of the Germanic Holy Roman Empire, midway through the 15th century, won the wrestling title of the Empire. One of the best wrestlers and fencing masters of his time, he wrote a wrestling compendium in which he separated for the first time wrestling from fencing. His system, called 'Ott'sches Ringen' is an important landmark in sports." [5]

As the memorial dedication allows us to presume that Ott is deceased by 1452, while the Encyclopaedia Judaica references a 16th century Ott, they either cannot be the same man or the Encyclopaedia entry's date must be inaccurate.

In another source even more specific information is given about Ott: "About the year 1500, Ott, a converted Jew, must have been a notable figure. Ott, who was known as the champion wrestler of Austria and who was the athletic adviser to the court of Frederick III, Emperor of the Germanic Holy Roman Empire, is the author of a book on wrestling."[6] Unfortunately in this secondary source we have, yet again, a mix of true, possibly true, and most certainly erroneous information. It would be lovely to know for certain that Ott was in the employ of Frederick III, but as of now this has not been confirmed. [7]

---

[4] Welle, Rainer, "…und wisse das alle hobischeit kompt von deme ringen", Translation by Christian Tobler.

[5] Ibid.

[6] Marcus, Jacob Rader, *The Rise and Destiny of the German Jew.*

[7] Welle, Rainer, "…und wisse das alle hobischeit kompt von deme ringen", p. 259.

We can say with a degree of certainty that Ott was baptized a Christian, as indicated by most of the treatises attributed to him. While it is unknown if this was a conversion under duress or one of the heart, it is interesting to speculate about his role in medieval society as a baptized Jew in the direct employ of German princes.

Unfortunately, other than these interesting scraps, little to nothing else is known of the man whose tradition of personal combat achieved enough fame to be recorded again and again by German martial arts masters throughout the next two centuries. If we cannot know details about Ott as a person, we can try to understand him through his presumed patrons and his place in the canon of medieval martial arts.

WRESTLER TO THE PRINCES OF AUSTRIA

In the copy found in the Von Danzig *Fechtbuch*, the prologue to Ott's work opens with, "Here begins the wrestling composed by Master Ott, God have mercy on him, who was a wrestler to the noble Princes of Austria." Paulus Kal referred to him as, in his list of deceased masters, a wrestler to the Lord of Austria.[8] What remains unclear is what, precisely, a "wrestling master" in Medieval Austria was, what their responsibilities were, and why Ott was set aside from other masters of the Art as being specifically a "wrestler." While information regarding Ott's specific employer or duties remains unknown, we can infer a lot of answers from the importance of wrestling in the courts of medieval Europe.

One source indicates that "there is evidence that matches between members of different classes were allowed in wrestling, for noblemen were quite proud of victories over powerful yeomen."[9] This direct competition between members of the noble class and the peasantry seems unique amongst all sports practiced in the middle ages. It may be that it is due to wrestling's special importance as a preparatory activity for soldiers from both the lower and upper orders that this intermingling was sometimes allowed and encouraged, though it must be noted there are also examples of these cross-class matches being specifically banned. Only in this context can we make sense of the fact that Ott, who as a baptized Jew was unlikely to hold any rank or title, was in the position of instructing young Christian lords in the art of wrestling.

---

[8] Tobler, Christian H., *In Service of the Duke*, p. 16.

[9] Morton, Gerald W. and O'Brien, George M., *Wrestling to 'Rasslin': Ancient Sport to American Spectacle*, p. 15-16.

In *Sports, Politics and Literature in the English Renaissance*, Gregory M. Colón Semenza discusses how wrestling matches seem to bridge the gap between classes in a way that other competitions do not:

> "…in Chaucer's Canterbury Tales, the competitive Miller who attempts to "quite" the Knight is described as a wrestler. Thought this fact has generally been overlooked as merely a sign of the Miller's boorish nature, his status as wrestler may actually be his most telling characteristic. In medieval and Renaissance England, wrestling - as we have seen - had both noble and plebian associations. Because the knight had to be skilled at hand-to-hand combat, much of his early training consisted of wrestling. For this reason, gentlemen often encouraged their young sons to compete in wrestling matches in order to prove their worth and bravery. Conversely, the wrestler who competed in matches for the sake of reward was a denigrated figure in medieval and renaissance England. The various feast days and holiday festivals, such as St. Bartholomew's Fair, offered non-nobles numerous opportunities to participate in wrestling matches for a prize. The fact that Chaucer's Miller is also a professional wrestler highlights his ambiguous social status."[10]

Conversely, Eric Dunning in *Sport: The Development of Sport* takes the position that "… aristocratic wrestling was probably quasi-private and overlaid with ceremonial trappings just as the martial and equestrian sports were." He goes further to say, "We cannot be sure that the literate bourgeoisie wrestled much," but concedes that with the printing of Fabian von Auerswald's *Ringerkunst* (1539) the intended audience was the rising "middle class".[11]

There were ample opportunities for the lower classes to wrestle, both in friendly matches, and competitively. While scholars of medieval life don't envision wrestling as being participated in by the average person,[12] it seems unlikely that with relatively few sporting opportunities, compared to today's proliferation of extracurricular activities, most boys would not have at least some grounding in this

[10] Colón Semenza, Gregory M., *Sports, politics, and literature in the English Renaissance*, p. 131.

[11] Dunning, Eric, *Sport: the Development of Sport*, p. 140.

[12] Newman, Paul B., *Daily Life in the Middle Ages*, p. 165 Newman asserts that "While written accounts of medieval wrestling are scarce, a few of the references indicate that wrestling matches were held as public entertainment and likely was more of a spectator sport than a participatory one for most people."

sport. One could draw an analogy between medieval wrestling and modern base-ball in the United States during the 1950s. While not all Americans were active players of the sport, most had played as a child if only in neighborhood pickup games. And even those that never or rarely played certainly understood the strate-gies and enjoyed watching games and following their favorite players.

Competitive wrestling matches were highly popular affairs in the Middle Ages, often held during feast days and even in church yards. There is an interesting ac-count in *The Chronicle of Jocelin of Brakelond,* a 12th century English manuscript, of a riot that occurs on Christmas Day between the townspeople and the Abbot's servants in 1197. The Abbot, entertainingly, suggests that further spetacula simply be held outside of the churchyard.[13] In another example, the Prioress of Clerken-well complained to King Edward I about damages to her fields caused by crowds who came to Clerkenwell to watch the wrestling matches (*luctas*) and miracle plays.[14]

In *Medieval London: Historical and Social,* Sir Walter Besant makes a comparison between wrestling and popular modern sports, emphasizing the unruly behavior that seemed to go hand-in-hand with wrestling matches. He writes, "The [medi-eval] wrestling match filled much the same place in the civic mind as the football match of the present day. It was not so much a sport as a battle, and occasionally … it caused serious riots and disturbances."[15] In fact, from the numerous ac-counts of rioting and wide-spread fighting associated with it, it seems "wrestling was a sport famous for the disorderliness it seemed to promote."[16]

While the lower classes might enjoy informal wrestling matches and compe-titions held on feast days, the upper classes certainly had their own wrestling competitions. An example of one of these is described by Morton and O'Brien in *Wrestling to Rasslin':* "The most famous such meet attended negotiations between Henry VIII and Francis I at a festival on the Field of the Cloth of Gold in 1520. As a part of the entertainment, seven wrestlers from each nation were matched up. The English won handily over the French who had failed to bring along their Breton champions. Accounts vary as to what followed. According to one version Henry gloated, Francis became so enraged that he jumped up and took hold of the English king. Attendants quickly separated the two monarchs. In another version, it is said that Henry challenged Francis who was five years his senior: "Brother, we

---

[13] McMurray Gibson, Gail, *The Theater of Devotion: East Anglican Drama and Society in the Late Middle Ages,* p. 114; 205.

[14] Hassall, W.O., "Plays at Clerkenwell", Modern Language Review, vol.33, 1938: 564-70.

[15] Besant, Walter, *Medieval London: Historical and Social,* p. 312.

[16] Semenza, Gregory M. Colón, *Historicizing 'Wrastlynge' in the Miller's Tale,* p. 70.

wolle wrestle." To save face the French king accepted. Henry gained quick advantage with his superior strength and athletic ability. But then, using his long legs to maneuver, Francis worked himself free and grabbing Henry's game leg pinned him. No second fall is recorded as the banquet table was set and waiting." [17]

Morton and O'Brien also hint at the duties of a medieval wrestling master, "As in other countries, an outstanding wrestler might catch the eye of his sovereign and join the royal retinue as a professional wrestler for courtly entertainment and international meets." [18]

Unfortunately, unless we find a personal account of one of these wrestling masters, we will not know what all of their duties entailed. It does seem likely, though, that they were both instructors of their noble patrons in the wrestling arts and personally represented their patron in high-stakes matches between members of the upper classes.

Wrestling Rules in Medieval Germany

Wrestling (*Ringen*) in a medieval context was not limited in technique to actions that occur in the grip. While modern people think of wrestling as being devoid of any strikes, there are a variety of strikes described in medieval treatises on wrestling, both punching and kicking. Due to this, there should not be an automatic assumption that all of the techniques are friendly or sporting in modern application.

It is somewhat unclear whether or not Ott's work can be considered sport-oriented. Certainly, we have seen that wrestling was a common sport across both class and geography in Europe during the Middle Ages. However, there was such variation of rules by time and place that it is impossible to say definitively whether or not the few destructive techniques described in Ott's work (breaks, wrenches and strikes) were intended to literally break a man's arm, or to put him in a position where he would submit from pain. It seems inconceivable that breaking a man's elbow or knee would be allowed in a friendly competition, especially considered in the light of the medical treatments available to men at this time. A dislocation of the elbow or break of the arm could easily be permanently disabling to a medieval man. One possible solution to this contradiction in terms is that while participating in a sporting engagement, the wrestler used these techniques to gain submission but reserved performing the actual break or dislocation for an antagonistic environment.

---

[17] Morton, Gerald W. and O'Brien, George M., *Wrestling to 'Rasslin': Ancient Sport to American Spectacle*, p 17.

[18] Ibid.

Regardless of whether bodily harm was intended to be done to a sporting opponent, or whether destructive techniques were employed, wrestling in the medieval period was a dangerous endeavor. Norman Wymer reminds us in *Sport in England* that the victor would only bear away the prize assuming "he was in a fit state to receive it, which was by no means certain in such times, when men would often wrestle against each other until one was dead and the other all but, if not completely, insensible."[19] Contemporary records support the idea that wrestling matches were sometimes fatal.

It must be considered that when discussing this as noble "sport" that it may have been as high-stakes as modern professional boxing or mixed martial arts, where men take massive punishment to their bodies, but where that risk is considered worth the relative payback of wealth and fame. We cannot say for certain that Ott's pay was on the equivalent level of today's professional athlete, but surely his compensation was significant, given that medieval English matches between peasants could net prizes of up to a month's salary. Unfortunately, at this time, I have been unable to unearth any wrestling rules that can be tied to Ott's Germany in both time and place. However it is certainly important to look at some contemporary examples that might to help us understand the types of rules that we might expect to see in 15th century Germany.

Morton and O'Brien describe medieval French wrestling matches thus: "The Bretons were especially noted for their strength and skill in a form of upright wrestling that allowed no grips below the waist, and no legholds or tripping. This is the origin of what eventually emerged as Greco-Roman wrestling....Because matches took place in public with women among the interested spectators, medieval wrestlers were fully clothed. The Bretons believed in fair sport. They met after making the sign of the cross, shook hands, promised to be friends whatever the outcome, and assured each other that they carried no magic charms and had not signed a pact with the devil to win."[20]

They describe a variety of English wrestling rules as well: "By the Middle Ages the Englishmen in various counties had developed different types of wrestling. The men of Lancashire preferred a loose or freestyle which is most similar to modern American amateur style in the initial stance taken, the great variety of holds and escapes employed, the pinning of both shoulders to determine victory.

---

[19] Wymer, Norman, *Sport in England: A History of Two Thousand Years of Games and Pastimes*, p. 23.

[20] Morton, Gerald W. and O'Brien, George M., *Wrestling to 'Rasslin': Ancient Sport to American Spectacle*, p. 15-16.

Kicking, grabbing of clothing or hair, pinching or punishing holds were prohibited. There is one variant of loose wrestling that was mainly an upright contest, for a man lost if any part of his body other than the feet, knees or hands touched the ground. In Devonshire and Cornwall, booted contestants started the bout with kicking, tripping and savate-like blows before locking up in close combat. Holds as in judo consisted in grasping the sleeve and the back of an opponent's jacket and then trying to toss him to the ground in a three-point landing; that is, both shoulder and one hip or one shoulder and both hips. In Cumberland and Westmoreland, backhold wrestling dating to the days of the Vikings was in vogue. Contestants took a stance with one arm over and one arm under the other man's shoulders. Hands remained locked behind the adversary's back as both struggled to toss or force the other to the ground. If a man lost his grip or if any part of his body other than the feet touched the ground, he lost the fall. If both fell to the ground at the same time, the fall was a 'dogfall' and had to be repeated."[21]

Richard Carew described a typical English wrestling match in his *Survey of Cornwall*, written in 1602. He says: "[T]he two champions set forth, stripped into their doublets and hosen, and untrussed, so that they may better command use of their lymmes; and first shaking hands, in token of friendship, they fall presently to the effect of anger; for each striveth how to take holde of the other with his beste advantage, and to beare his adverse party downe."[22]

These few examples show what a great variety of rulesets may have existed in just one, fairly homogenous country, illustrating the difficulty in proclaiming a "definitve" set of rules for an area as large and diverse as the Holy Roman Empire.

We can get further hints at what wrestling matches might have looked like from other sources. In the *Etymologies* of Isidore of Seville, St. Isidore describes wrestling: "Some suppose that the art of wrestling was revealed by the fighting of bears, for among all the beasts they alone stand erect in their grappling, and quickly crouch and turn back, and by turns sometimes attack with their paws and sometimes avoid grappling, in the manner of wrestlers."[23]

The most telling pieces of evidence regarding how Ott intends his wrestling to be used can be gleaned from his treatise. When considered against the larger body of work on medieval German wrestling techniques, there are some conspicuous absences. First, Ott does not detail any work on the ground, such as pins or holds. This implies that the situation he was writing for did not include this groundwork. Perhaps his contests, like the wrestling of Devonshire and Cornwall described

---

[22] Carew, Richard, *Survey of Cornwall*, p. 75.

[23] Barney, Stephen A., et al, *The Etymologies of Isidore of Seville, by St. Isidore (of Seville)*, p. 366.

above, were fought to the third fall and did not continue to the ground. Second, Ott also does not include the kicks and strikes outlined in other German wrestling treatises, nor does he describe any actions outside of a grip to the body or arms. It seems, then, that this obvious exclusion indicates a contest that requires beginning from a grip.

We can, then, reasonably guess that a wrestling contest in medieval Germany might have been held within a circular boundary of a certain size (10-15' diameter was common across time and place) and begun with a handshake or bow and perhaps another sign of goodwill such as making the sign of the cross. They may be entirely clothed, stripped to their underwear, or possibly nude.[24] They would then gain a grip upon their opponent's arms or body, the specifics of which would be determined by their particular wrestling strategy. They would then attempt to throw their opponent off of his feet in order to gain a score. They would then reset and begin again, until one or the other had performed three throws on his opponent. It seems likely that the match would end with another sign of goodwill.

OTHER WRESTLING IN THE GERMAN MATERIALS

No matter how central Ott's treatise was to the fightbook authors, it is important to remember that the techniques shown in Ott are not the entirety of the German corpus of material on the subject and that there are differences in the various manuscripts that imply differing focuses. For instance, within the Ringeck (Dresd. C 487) manuscript there are anonymous treatises on wrestling that include *Unterhalten* (or "Holding Down") techniques as well as *Mortstoß* ("Murder-Stikes", which include punching the body, neck and face and kicks to the genitals), none of which are found in Ott's work. These treatises might have been intended for sporting contests with different rule sets, but I suspect that they were intended for self-defense or combative purposes. No matter how tough and pain-tolerant medieval man may have been, it seems unlikely that any sporting contest would open with a knee to the testicles.

The Ringeck compendium also contains a number of other treatises on wrestling, only one of which is a copy of Ott, and that an unattributed copy of only the second half of Ott's work. Codex Wallerstein (Cod.I.6.40.2), another large medieval treatise on combat, contains an extensive wrestling section, and yet the techniques seem to only be cursorily related to Ott's techniques. In fact, nearly every

---

[24] While illustrated *fechtbucher* do not show nude or partially dressed examples, manuscript marginalia often shows men in their underwear, and as Semenza reports in *Historicizing 'Wrastlynge" in the Miller's Tale*: "when Bertrand du Guesclin's (1320-1380) aunt learned of her nephew's most recent wrestling victories, she is reported to have asked, 'How can a nobleman of seventeen fight naked with those serfs in the market place?'"

manual on swordsmanship contains wrestling techniques, be they with weapon in hand, while wearing armour or when completely unarmed. This is a large body of work which includes a wide-ranging variety of techniques. Yet, within this large corpus, Ott appears to be relatively selective in the techniques he shows, limiting himself to throws and very few limb wrenches/breaks, whereas the larger corpus seems to show many more destructive techniques, strikes, kicks and breaks. In some ways, this seems reminiscent of the similarities and differences between modern judo and classical jujutsu, where one art (judo, in this case) focuses on a subset of techniques from a broader art (jujutsu). This is not to say that one art is lacking when compared to another, but rather that their focus is different for a variety of societal reasons.

While I will often cross-reference Kal and Talhoffer's works on wrestling with Ott's work in the interpretive section of this work, this does not mean that the techniques shown in these manuscripts are identical or derived from Ott's work on the subject. Rather, they simply seem to have the most related material of the illustrated manuals and are, therefore, easy to associate for the purpose of visualizing the techniques from a medieval example.

Wrestling in the Greater Art

While this work is focused on Ott's treatise and the wrestling contained within it, it is important to keep in mind that wrestling, in a medieval context, was not limited to unarmed actions within a circle of friendly combat. Wrestling techniques are used in conjunction with all of the weapons of the *Kunst des Fechten*, most notably the dagger.

Techniques using the dagger often involve a cover of some kind, protecting you from his dagger, followed by a wrestling throw and further work from that place of domination. This "wrestling with a dagger" was not limited to self-defense techniques, but also was used in encounters where both combatants were wearing entire suits of armor. Again, the general idea seems to be that it's easier to deal with an opponent who is laying flat on the ground than if he's standing in ready defense. Some of these techniques are identical to some of Ott's throws, though there are specialized throws which use either your dagger or his own armor against the opponent. While understanding and practice of the more specialized techniques is certainly useful, having a strong working knowledge of the basics of medieval wrestling goes a long way to making dagger play flow easily in or out of armor.

This benefit extends out to all other weapon forms. Wrestling knowledge is helpful for those studying the longsword, for example, because anytime an opponent enters uncovered into grappling range you can use your understanding of balance and timing against him to throw him off his feet, regardless of the sword in his hand. Similarly, there are wrestling techniques shown in treatises on messer, sword and buckler, spear, poleaxe, and armored sword combat.

In this way, even students of the Art who are concentrating their attention and study on a single weapon or subset of techniques should additionally study and understand wrestling. Without this knowledge, a student of the sword limits themself to fighting only in certain ranges and will be at the mercy of one who knows how to fight at wrestling range.

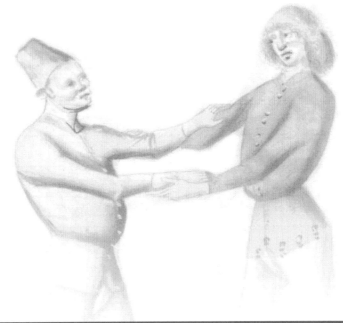

3

ORGANIZATION OF OTT'S TREATISE

One of the most frustrating problems a modern practitioner faces when beginning to learn Ringen techniques from Ott's treatise is that his techniques are not necessarily presented in an order conducive to learning the material quickly. The first half of the treatise is in a seemingly logical order, first teaching wrestling at the arms, then a counter technique which counters all actions at the arms, and then finally wrestling techniques at the body. Unfortunately, after that the second-half of the treatise presents techniques which are in no discernable order. In fact, some of the techniques in the "second-half" are counters for techniques in the "first-half", making it difficult to work with as written.

Interestingly, that "second-half" of techniques are actually presented alone in the Ringeck manuscript and in that work are not attributed to Ott at all, but are rather simply titled "Other Good Wrestling Techniques and Counters."[25] This begs the question, particularly paired with the tight organization of the techniques previous to this section, if this is Ott's work at all. It could be that this second half is in fact the work of another anonymous wrestling master. Or, it could be that

---

[25] Ringeck (78r ff.)

Ott was simply not attributed in Ringeck. Or it could even be that Ott had written two separate treatises in previous, currently unknown, works that were later consolidated in the Von Danzig manuscript and copied thereafter in the remaining manuscripts that present his work. At this time, we simply must assume that it's Ott's work which for some reason seems to change "voice" part way through the manuscript.

The techniques attributed to Ott, as recorded in Von Danzig and Ringeck, are broken down in a seemingly random way; jumping back and forth between categories of techniques:

> **Von Danzig:**
> Prologue
> 17 techniques at the arms
> 6 techniques at the body
>
> **Von Danzig and Ringeck – From this point onwards the manual is the same in both texts**
> 1 technique at the arms
> 1 technique if he grasps you from behind
> 1 technique at the arms
> 2 techniques at the body
> 3 techniques at the arms
> 2 techniques at the body
> 2 techniques at the arms
> 1 technique if he grasps you from behind
> 1 technique at the body
> 1 technique at the arms
> 5 techniques at the body
> 1 technique at the arms
> 2 techniques for when he has grasped you from behind
> 3 techniques involving a grip to the collar
> 1 technique at the arms

4

OTT'S PROLOGUE
AND FIGHT THEORY

N early all of the existent examples of Master Ott's treatise open with a prologue, which provides succinct advice as to how one should approach a
fight. We are told that there are three virtues of wrestling: Skill, Quickness and Strength.

Ott ties the concept of initiative in a wrestling match to the relative strength or
weakness of an opponent. This concept of initiative is central to the philosophy
behind the wider martial arts of the Liechtenauer tradition, and more than any-
thing, establishes Ott's position as a member of the "Society of Liechtenauer".
Generally, the idea is that if one has initiative, that is if one is the actor, then they
will win the engagement as their opponent will be forced to react and in that position of reacting will make a, presumably, fatal mistake. Masters of Liechtenauer's
art describe initiative as being broken down into three times, *Vor*, *Nach* and *Indes*.
Acting in the *Vor* is acting before our opponent, or controlling our opponent's
actions by presenting him with a situation that has only limited options available
to him. Acting in the *Nach*, or after, is to react to our opponent's motion or to a
threat he is presenting. *Indes*, the third time, is difficult to translate but works out
to something like "during" or "simultaneously." The key to understanding and

excelling in Liechtenauer's Art is to know how to use *Indes* to move from being the reactor to the actor; to move from *Nach* to *Vor*.

> **Here begins the wrestling composed by Master Ott, God have mercy on him, who was wrestling teacher to the noble Prince of Austria.**

> **In all wrestling there should be three things. The first is skill. The second is quickness. The third is the proper application of strength. Concerning this, you should know that the best is quickness, because it prevents him from countering you. Thereafter you should remember that you should wrestle a weaker man in the Before [Vor], an equal opponent simultaneously, and a stronger man in the After [Nach]. In all wrestling in the Before, attend to quickness; in all simultaneous wrestling, attend to the balance [Waage]; and in all wrestling in the After, attend to the crook of the knee. [26]**

This assessment of our opponent's relative strength can be done either before we meet in a grip, allowing us to develop a game plan of how to approach an opponent and which techniques are likely to give one success, or can (and should!) be done on the fly as the grip develops and pressures are applied. If your opponent is strong in the grip, and has placed you in the *Nach* you can then "attend to the crook of the knee" as Ott tells us to do. We can see all of the advice from his prologue play out time and again in his presentation of the techniques.

It is important to consider for a moment weaker and stronger opponents and how Ott's advice plays into commonly-held understandings about wrestling. When one opponent is greatly weaker than the other, the stronger man can, by dint of weight, move the weaker man around. He simply has the ability to bring greater force to the grip, and therefore shift the balance in whatever direction he chooses. But this does not mean that the stronger man automatically wins. For those familiar with longsword techniques, we could draw a parallel between the grip in wrestling and the bind between two swords. When dealing with a longsword bind, we are advised by masters of the sword to use Weakness against Strength and vice-versa. This is the way that one can control the bind and achieve one's goals. How one uses Weakness against Strength is best described by Jigoro

---

[26] Von Danzig.

Kano, the founder of judo. He is quoted as saying in the introduction to judo in the 1932 Olympics at the University of Southern California:[27]

> "Suppose we assume that we may estimate the strength of a man in units of one. Let us say that the strength of a man standing in front of me is represented by ten units, whereas my strength, less than his, is represented by seven units. Then if he pushes me with all his force, I shall certainly be pushed back or thrown down, even if I use all my strength against him. This would happen because I used all my strength against him, opposing strength to strength. But if, instead of opposing him, I were to give way to strength by withdrawing my body just as much as he had pushed, remembering to keep my balance, then he would naturally lean forward and thus lose his balance. In this new position, he may have become so weak (not in actual physical strength, but because of his awkward position) as to have his strength represented for the moment by, say, only three units only instead of his normal ten units. But meanwhile I, by keeping my balance, retain my full strength, as originally represented by seven units. Here then, I am momentarily in a advantageous position, and I can defeat my opponent by using only half of my strength, that is half of my seven units, or three and one-half of my strength against his three. This leaves one-half of my strength available for any other purpose. In case I had greater strength than my opponent, I could of course push him back. But even in this case, that is, if I had wished to push him back and had the power to do so, it would be better for me to have given way, because in doing so I should have greatly economized my energy."

Kano, in his example, shows how one can be both strong in muscle and weak in the grip. It is important when considering Ott's advise to apply it to both of these scenarios.

---

[27] Kobayashi, Kiyoshi and Sharp, Harold, "The Sport of Judo" p. vi-vii.

It is interesting to compare and contrast Ott's prologue to the prologue in the Codex Wallerstein:[28]

The First Lesson of Wrestling[29] (from Codex Wallerstein)

Item: It should be noted that wrestling should have three things - strength, measure, and nimbleness. Strength is needed so that one can go low into the balance and be strongly positioned on the earth; measure so that you can properly use your hands and feet in all stances, as you will learn hereafter; and nimbleness, so that you perform well all the stepping behind, pulling, punching, and arm breaks and remember them well so you can employ all these things quickly and always with power, and come into the balance.

There are many similarities, and while the techniques seem to be related, there are some marked differences in the apparent wrestling strategy between these two treatises. A comparison of Ott's work contrasted to the work in Codex Wallerstein is beyond the scope of this writing, but is an important data point that should be taken up by a researcher. This shouldn't be surprising, because as we have seen, wrestling has a long and illustrious history filled with local custom and technique. Each hamlet seemed to have its own specific rules or techniques based on those rules. However, with a prologue as seemingly original as Ott's, it begs the question if the author of Codex Wallerstein borrowed the prologue from Ott, or if there was a common source, now lost. Perhaps these concepts were well-known and accepted basics of wrestling that were orally passed on from wrestler to wrestler? Sadly, we'll likely never know for sure.

---

[28] Anonymous, Fechtbuch (after 1400). Cod. I.6.4º.2, Universitätsbibliothek Augsburg, Augsburg, Germany.

[29] From Codex Wallerstein, translation by Christian Tobler, 2011.

Wrestling at the body is a poor tactical choice for the much smaller man.

USING THE FIGHT THEORY

One of the most important strategic considerations for wrestling an opponent is their relative weight and strength. While modern wrestling matches are set up between like opponents, that is, those who weigh within a few pounds of each other, it does not seem likely that this was the case in medieval Europe. As such, it would then be important for each wrestler to understand which techniques are likely to best serve him against a mismatched opponent. As an entertaining example of the importance of this strategic thinking, consider for a moment the pairing of Westley and Fezzik in "The Princess Bride." Wrestling at the Body is clearly a poor choice for the smaller man in this match.

Rather, Ott tells us that the smaller man should act in the *Nach* (that is after his opponent commits to a movement) and attend to the knee (referencing a subset of throws where you pick up a leg to drop a man on his back). Tellingly, in one technique where Ott describes how to gain a grip at the body under his arms, he pairs this instruction with the assessment "if he is small and you can well lift him." It would have served Westley well to first consider his relative strength before gaining this grip!

When assessing our opponent to determine if he is weaker or stronger than ourselves once we have come to grips, we find that we must use that ever-present concept of *Fühlen* about which Master Liechtenauer and the author of the anonymous gloss in Von Danzig says:

> **Learn the feeling. The word Instantly slices sharply.**
>
> **Gloss – Note: "Feeling" and the word "Instantly" are the greatest and best of the art of the sword. And anyone who is or wants to be a master of the sword and does not understand the Feeling, and has not also learnt the word "Instantly", is not a master, but a Büffel[30] at the sword. Therefore, before all else, you should learn these two things well so that you understand them truly. [31]**

Fühlen means "feeling" and it is a skill that is described across the entire Art, regardless of the weapon in hand. It is through *Fühlen* that we know which technique to use in the moment.

As a wrestler, you should work to learn to sense your opponent's intent through your contact with his body. If you hold him at the arms, you should learn to feel if he's pulling you forwards, pushing you backwards, twisting or withdrawing in some manner. The sooner you are able to feel these impulses, the more time you will have to act to counter his action. This is something that can only be learned through practice and time in the grip. As noted above, anyone who does not understand the feeling is not a master.

---

[30] A buffalo; that is, a clod who relies purely upon brute strength.

[31] Von Danzig, in Tobler, *In St. George's Name*, p. 124.

5

BASIC WRESTLING

I t is beyond the scope of this book to instruct a student on all of the intricacies of wrestling. Many important life lessons are simply best learned face-to-face, rather than from a book, and I strongly believe that wrestling is foremost amongst these. While I will do my best to describe actions through the written word and still photo, some things simply must be felt to be understood.

Though this book is focused on medieval wrestling and has a few oddities related to that, I highly encourage anyone who is serious about the pursuit of medieval wrestling to get a good physical background with any number of modern wrestling arts, be it judo, jujutsu, collegiate wrestling, or some other type of wrestling that you may have access to locally. A single one-hour session with a wrestling coach will teach you more than you could learn in twenty hours of only training with a book.

HOW TO PRACTICE

BE SAFE

The most important piece of wrestling practice is safety.

All students are intuitively aware, when handed a weapon, that they have the potential to do damage to their training partners and will usually drill carefully, often even without being told to do so. Sometimes, they will do so to their own detriment and have to be coached out of practicing ineffectively for the fear of doing harm!

Not so with wrestling. Most of us grew up wrestling (usually in a most informal and playful manner) with our fathers, friends and siblings and an internal memory of this remains with us all. What we often don't realize, however, is that in the intervening years we have grown bigger, stronger and taller…all of which lead to the potential to do more harm. People who don't have much wrestling experience perceive it as just "good fun" and not for what it is: a combative, potentially lethal art. If you sense that you, or your training partner, is mentally "checking out" and is no longer drilling safely then step back and take a moment to reset. Training is not the time to disengage your brain!

If you do not have access to good wrestling mats or do not have extensive experience falling, it is important that you do not practice these throws to completion. It is possible (and important) to spend time practicing the entry and setup to throws as well as learning to break the opponent's balance. In this way you can practice wrestling until you have access to the proper equipment.

Be Clean

Special emphasis on cleanliness is important when you wrestle. Have respect for yourself, your training partner, and the Art being studied, by assuring that you attend practice with a clean body and uniform. Fingernails and toenails (if training shoeless) should be kept short. Long hair should be tied back and kept out of one's face and off of one's neck. Jewelry – rings, watches, earrings or piercings – need to be removed as they are risks for serious injury to both parties.

Work Hard

Practice should be hard! Many of the concepts in wrestling will simply not work if you laze about, chatting with your partner, and only practice the throw half-heartedly. Every partner has something to teach you and you can't learn it if you're too busy talking. If you become genuinely confused, ask an instructor for clarification, or if you're training on your own, move on and look for clarification at another time. Practice is your chance to get physical answers to your questions!

That said if you are truly fatigued, slow down. Over fatigue is also detrimental, as your body and mind won't be able to operate properly. If you are injured, use your good judgment to decide how hard you should push yourself at practice.

If in Doubt, don't Complete

When you are throwing a partner, and you aren't entirely sure that it's a safe throw, *do not complete it!* If you're not sure of the point of a particular drill, do not complete it. If your partner seems to have mentally "checked out", do not complete your throw.

If your partner is not expecting to be countered in a drill, ***do not counter their throw***.

Because medieval wrestling was not necessarily limited to actions from the grip, proper safety measures and training equipment should be considered. Some of the throws and techniques shown in Ott's treatise involve the application of pain, be it via pressure to the throat, eyes or face, or a joint lock. Nearly all of them can be modified in such a way that they can be used in modern friendly competition. But, more often than not, students are drilling these techniques in the way they are written, against a mostly compliant partner.

The trouble comes in when we have a non-compliant partner. They can be non-compliant for any number of reasons; but competitiveness and surprise are the two biggest sources of non-compliance that occur in practice. When you apply a throw via a joint lock against someone who is not expecting it, chances are it will work in a dramatic way, leading to an injury that can range from irritating to debilitating to crippling.

Think before applying a technique and always practice with your head in the game.

Falling Safely

Falling is one of the most important tools that you will need to have in order to be able to practice safely. You need to be able to fall in any direction confidently and correctly in order to prevent injuries. It will also allow you to practice techniques more completely as you won't be concerned about taking a fall.

With all falls, it is important that you balance tension and relaxation in your body as you come to the ground. You must be relaxed so that you are able to absorb the shock of hitting the ground without jarring or shocking your body. At the same time, hitting the ground like a sack of wet noodles does little for your martial preparation to continue to fight as you go to the ground. An important balance must be struck between these two extremes of tension.

As you learn to fall and roll, it is important to remember to coordinate your breath with your fall. Exhale as you go to the ground – this will help keep you from the feeling of having the wind knocked out of you as well as naturally contracting your core, providing the protective tension required to fall safely. Another key point is that you should endeavor to have your arms follow your body to the ground. It is quite easy to break a wrist or arm if you attempt to catch yourself as you fall so you should train until you have overcome this common reflex.

FALLING BACKWARDS

FIRST

- ❖ Start from a squatting position with the arms extended forwards

- ❖ Start to fall back, keeping your chin well tucked by looking at your feet.

- ❖ As your rear touches the ground, let your legs come up. Just as your back begins to touch the mat, let your arms come naturally to your sides with a space between your arms and body. Keep your arms relaxed, do not stiffen them.

- ❖ Roll onto your well-rounded back

- ❖ IMPORTANT: Stay relaxed. Take it easy at first until you become more confident.

NEXT

- ❖ From a standing position, take a few steps backwards and start to squat, falling backwards.

- ❖ Keep the chin well-tucked. Go through the same motions outlined above.

FALLING TO THE SIDE

FIRST

- ❖ Start by squatting low on one leg, extending the other across and in front of you. Raise the arm on the side where your leg is extended (this is the side you will fall onto).

- ❖ Keep the chin well-tucked, again by looking at your feet.

- ❖ Allow yourself to fall to the side, with a rounded body and the extended arm coming naturally to the ground.

NEXT

- ❖ From a standing position, slide one foot across the ground in front of you. As you do this, raise the arm on the same side.

- ❖ Keep the chin tucked.

- ❖ Begin to squat and as your rear end comes near to your foot, allow yourself to fall to the side with a relaxed and rounded body. The fall will be from a slightly higher place. The extended arm comes naturally to the ground.

FALLING FORWARDS

FIRST

- ❖ Kneel on the floor, arms extended forwards and with soft elbows.

- ❖ Allow your body to fall forwards, keeping your body straight and landing on your hands and bending your elbows to come to your forearms.

NEXT

- ❖ From a standing position, extend your arms forward.

- ❖ Allow your body to fall forwards, keeping your body straight, and landing on your hands forearms, ending as if in a plank position.

ROLLING BACKWARDS

FIRST

- ❖ Start from a squatting position with the arms extended forwards.

- ❖ Start to fall back, keeping your chin well tucked by looking at your feet.

- ❖ As your rear touches the ground, let your legs come up. Just as your back begins to touch the mat, let your arms come naturally to your sides with a space between your arms and body.

- ❖ Roll onto your well-rounded back and allow your momentum to carry you in a reverse somersault. This motion should be focused over one shoulder, not across your head/neck. You will end on all fours, facing forwards.

NEXT

- ❖ Start from a squatting position with the arms extended forwards.

- ❖ Start to fall back, keeping your chin well tucked by looking at your feet.

- ❖ As your rear touches the ground, let your legs come up. Just as your back begins to touch the mat, let your arms come naturally to your sides with a space between your arms and body.

- ❖ Roll onto your well-rounded back and allow your momentum to carry you in a reverse somersault. Push against the ground with your straightened arm to propel your body with more vigorous force. This motion should be focused over one shoulder, not across your head/neck! Come up onto your knees or feet, allowing your hands to come up off the floor and into a ready position.

ROLLING FORWARDS

FIRST

❖ Start from a crouched position, with your hands on the ground in front of you. Turn one hand on the ground so that it points between your legs. This will make the elbow of that hand face forwards and will assist you in tucking the lead shoulder. This is important so that it will not hit the ground. The other arm should be in a natural position, hand pointing in the direction you are facing.

❖ Keep your chin tucked at all times.

❖ Push with your legs, keeping your back rounded, so that you roll across the floor, not "back-flopping" against it. You should roll over the lead shoulder and end up on the other side, that is, if you begin with your left arm, you end up on your right side.

❖ IMPORTANT: Stay relaxed. Take it easy at first until you become more confident.

NEXT

❖ Start from a standing position.

❖ Reach out with your inverted arm, curving it so that it points between your legs. Step with the same-side leg.

❖ Tuck your chin and push off with your toes, so that you somersault across your lead shoulder. You should roll over the lead shoulder and end up rolling across your right hip.

❖ Allow your momentum to continue, rolling until you are in a standing position.

6

STANCE AND GRIPS

Throughout the wrestling world there are a variety of ways that wrestlers stand, approach one another, and gain a grip on each other. This can depend on a variety of elements which includes the rules of the engagement, the required clothing (or lack thereof!), the individual wrestler's preference or strategic choice, or even the environment where the match is being held. For brevity and clarity, in this book we have chosen to adopt an upright stance based on the images shown in Paulus Kal's treatise, though it could be argued that other stances might be used depending on the above-mentioned specifics of a martial encounter.

 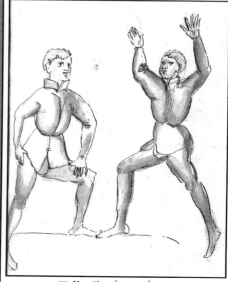

Talhoffer (1449) 35r

How to Stand when not in a grip

You should assume a natural stance, with either your right or left foot leading and your weight balanced slightly towards the front foot. Ott gives us no direction regarding the stance, but Talhoffer (1449) shows two stances before the grip.

One stance (left) is done with the hands held low and before the thighs. The other (right) is with the hands held high above the head on either side. Both have advantages and weaknesses, much like any guard, and should be practiced so that both are familiar.

A later master, Fabian Von Auerswald, also shows these two stances, albeit with a much subtler difference between the two stances. He includes, however, the advice:

> **First, look to see if he comes at you high or low. If he goes high, you mustn't allow yourself to fear, and can draw freely from these techniques, as your inclinations dictate. However, if he goes low, then be more cautious.**

In a manuscript copy of Von Auerswald's work, there are additional notes and instructions accompanying the illustrated plates, and the anonymous author's advice related to the approach to the grip and to begin wrestling is invaluable:

First, see if your opponent goes high or low. If he goes high, then you shouldn't worry and perform the plays that you can freely perform on him. If he goes low, then you have to pay good attention to him.

Fabian von Auerswald (1539), Plate 4

Secondly, one should pay diligent attention to whether one comes with outstretched limbs or crooked. The one who comes to another with extended limbs is easiest to bring to weakness and thereafter subdue, particularly when one knows to grasp the weak points or joints of the body: the hands and feet, whichever part of the body is closest; thereafter also the entire body, the neck, the genitals, and both places, behind or under the ears.

Thirdly, one should pay good attention to whether one comes to the other with a closed or open body. When he comes with a closed body, then you must have a lot of trouble before you can unlock his body. If he comes though with an outstretched and open body, then you can attack him very boldly in the weak spots. All of these things must be considered in this figure by the author of this book, who wears the plain clothing, standing with lowly dress and lowered body, with bent and drawn together joints, with closed body and hands. Thus he cannot easily be brought from his advantage, nor as easily harmed in the extremities' weakness or thrown to the ground as his opponent.[32]

---

[32] von Auerswald, Fabian, Ringer Kunst: fünff und achtzig stücke zu ehren Kurfürstlichen gnaden zu Sachsen etc. VD 16 A 4051, Georg-August-Universität Göttingen, Göttingen, Germany. Translation by Christian H. Tobler, 2012.

It is certainly easier to read an opponent's intentions that come at you high, for there are only a few things that he might try from this position. Von Auerswald references the sense of *Fühlen* discussed above when he says "as your inclinations dictate" telling us that we should, before all else, sense what the opponent will do.

NOTES

❖ Stand with your feet slightly apart and one leg leading. Your weight should be fairly evenly distributed between the feet and slightly on the balls of your feet. You should feel prepared to step in any direction with either of your feet at any time.

❖ Hold your hands before your thighs or above your head to either side. An important part of this advice is to keep your hands and arms out of attacking space until you need bring them to bear. If you enter with a hand forward, your opponent can grab that hand and use it to bring you to a technique before you have a grip on him. It is better to shoot the hand out when you are in range to grab the opponent than to enter his grasping range exposed.

❖ Your back should be erect, head up, shoulders back. As with the hands, it is important to enter into grappling range without giving him your head as the first thing to enter this distance. Maintaining an upright posture denies him this control point.

❖ Do not brace your body! Beginners tend to be stiff due to fear, uncertainty and awkwardness. If you are stiff, you will be unable to effectively read your opponent in the grip. Be relaxed while upright. Check in with your posture frequently by shaking out the arms and shoulders, as well as rolling your head, to make sure you aren't bringing unneeded tension into your stance.

How to Move

Though Ott's work does not include punches and kicks, it is important to remember that these techniques are included in the greater medieval wrestling corpus and therefore it is advisable to get into the habit of entering into distance prepared to cover against a punch. The covers and how to throw once you have achieved cover is explored extensively in the dagger treatises in the medieval tradition. While they are closely related, it is beyond the scope of this work to fully explore these covers and counters. Simply keep in mind that while we will learn these techniques from a grip, that getting those grips aren't necessarily a simple manner of walking up to your man and grabbing his arms, depending on the situation. Rather, to fully explore close-quarters combat in the medieval tradition you will need to study further medieval works on the dagger, the *Mortstoß*, and the *Unterhalten*.

If you choose to limit your techniques to those shown in Ott's treatise and interpreted in this book, you may want to eliminate the option of punches or kicks from your practice. As some medieval rules for sport wrestling clearly do not allow strikes it is reasonable to do so. Further, this concentration on the canonical grip and plays deriving from the grip can be helpful to new students to the art of wrestling.

Stepping

Stepping into distance can be done either with passing (changing lead foot) or gathered steps (maintaining lead foot) as well as a variety of crossing steps, pivots, box steps or compass steps. We aren't given explicit instruction with regards to what steps to use with each throw and I think this is because the answer depends on what position each wrestler is in. Without this foreknowledge Ott can't say precisely how we should step, but he can tell us where to step relative to our opponent's body and this is what's most important to a throw. The two most important steps are the passing step and the gathered step, as they allow us to position our body around our opponent according to the instructions.

A passing step is little more than a walking step, whereby one foot passes the other. In a wrestling context, you might find it useful to sink your weight a little by bending your knees slightly and making somewhat shorter steps than you might in another context. As you enter to wrestle, a passing step will allow you to alter the side of the body you have forwards and therefore which side of your opponent you will be attacking. You can also use this passing footwork to change which side you are holding in the grip at the arms. Finally, passing footwork is used to step behind the opponent to power many different throws.

A gathered step is a type of step where you do not change lead legs, but rather maintain your current posture. This can be done two different ways, by stepping forward with your lead leg, then gathering up the back leg, or by gathering up the back leg and the springing forward with the lead leg. Both have their place in a wrestler's repertoire. The important thing to remember is that during the brief moment when your feet are either too far apart or too close together your balance is not at its optimum which could leave you open to a savvy opponent. This is one of the many reasons that it is important to break your opponent's balance as you enter, but before committing yourself with footwork, as will be discussed in the following section.

Depending on what the technique requires, you may need to step slightly or largely, inside his feet or outside, and you may need to be able to turn around quickly. It is important to practice all of these types of movements alone in a solo drill and while in grip with a partner. As you practice these movements, be aware of your balance and the balance between you and your opponents in the grip. You want to maintain a neutral position in your own body and between you and your opponent right up until the point that you're ready to attack. Do not commit yourself too far forwards or backwards for this will give him an opening to exploit. It is important to be able to modulate your footwork to match your opponent's footwork, no matter what it is. An important part of wrestling is to be able to flow with an opponent as much as to oppose him.

BREAKING THE OPPONENT'S BALANCE

Breaking your opponent's balance is a core concept to all standing wrestling. It is the first thing that must happen before any attempt to throw can occur. There are a number of ways to break an opponent's balance, but the simplest is the method you will use when training wrestling techniques in drills with a semi-compliant partner.

When you wish to throw your opponent straight over your back, such as in a Forward Hip Throw (Page 72), it is important that you break his balance straight forwards before you step to enter into body contact with him. This is because you will be momentarily exposed during your step and vulnerable to a counter in that moment. To prevent his counter, you must make him unable to move effectively because he has already begun to fall. This is what it means to break someone's balance: to put them in a position where they would have to step to prevent themselves from falling.

In the case of the throw I have already mentioned, you would pull hard on his left arm, straight towards yourself, which will pull his weight onto the balls of his feet and maybe even hard enough that his rear foot is beginning to leave the ground. If you did nothing else at this point, he would have to step some way in order recapture his balanced posture. In this moment is your opening to attack with your throw.

It sometimes happens that as you attempt to pull someone off balance, they sink their weight and prevent themselves from being pulled. Now, in this moment, you can off-balance them by changing your pull to a push, and shifting from a Forward Hip Throw as your attack to a Shoulder-Knee Rear Throw (page 66). This would be an example of a "combination throw" where you attack with one throw to get the desired response, then move on to a prepared attack in another direction.

It is in this concept of the push-pull of breaking balance where we can really see the wisdom of Ott's prologue. He tells us that in the *Indes* of the fight we are to attend to the balance, and it is this concept of being prepared to shift your weight from one side to the other as necessary that will be the determining factor of who wins an exchange.

When breaking an opponent's balance, it can be helpful to think of the grip between yourself and your opponent as being similar to pulling on a slackened rope. You

Jessica breaks Aron's balance forward by pulling on his jacket near his shoulders, rocking his weight onto his toes.

Jessica breaks Aron's balance backward by pushing on his upper chest, sending his weight to his heels.

want to be able to pull smoothly, not snapping the rope taut, but instead bringing it to tension and then continuing the pull through. If you jerk his arm, he will feel that 'snap' and will react instinctively backwards and opposite the way you want him to go. When the pull is done steadily and with skill, the opponent doesn't realize he is being pulled off-balance until he's already falling into place for your throw.

To break an opponent, it is important that you maintain your own good balance through the action. Do not use leaning to power the action, but rather use the turning of your body and footwork to power it. In the example above, the pull on his left arm is powered by turning the torso and shoulders as you push upwards on his right arm with your left hand to break him free on that side. This pull with the right while pushing with the left should bring him onto his left foot if he has a left-leg lead or will pull him onto both toes and into open space if he has a right leg lead. Now you are free to step before his feet with your left foot, which also untwists your torso and sets you square before him to throw him over your hip.

Breaking balance is a vital skill for any wrestler. It can be trained in solo drills by pulling on resistance cords wrapped around a solid object, in paired drills by pulling and pushing opponents in time with their movements, and finally against a resistant opponent by trying to make them step against their will

NOTES

❖ It is imperative that you break your opponent's balance before you try to throw him.

❖ If you wish to move your opponent, do so by moving your body.

❖ If your opponent moves you, do not resist strongly, go with him. If you resist, your body becomes stiff and it's easier to lose your balance. By moving with your opponent, it's easier to control his body and unbalance him.

❖ It is always easier to throw an opponent in the direction he moves.

❖ Balance can be broken forwards or backwards, to the right or left, and combinations of both.

GENERAL NOTES ON THROWING

Throwing is the capstone which rests upon all of the previous steps. If you have maintained your balance, used correct footwork, and remain upright in your stepping then the throw will happen as a matter of course.

Almost all throws can be made with a rotation of the body and very little bending down. In order to facilitate this, look to the place you want to throw your opponent, then 'point' there with your arms, which will assist in the rotational aspect of the throw. Using the previous example of the Forward Hip Throw, the completion occurs by maintaining the pull with your right arm on his left arm. This will pull his upper body over your hip on your left side. As you pull, push with your left arm and corkscrew your body, straightening your legs to "pop" him into the air. You may slightly bend down as a natural movement, but again, you shouldn't think of bending over to take him down but rather striking him to the ground.

NOTES

❖ All techniques can be done from right or left side, but will be shown from the right in this book. Simply reverse directions to train the left side.

❖ Avoid bending at the waist, bending at the knees instead.

❖ KEEP YOUR BODY RELAXED. This will conserve energy, make it harder for your opponent to throw you and will not telegraph your intent to your opponent.

❖ Do not attempt a half-hearted throw. Weak attempts are wastes of energy and will not teach you what you're trying to learn, nor will they give your partner the opportunity to feel that throw in the grip.

❖ Keep your body close to your opponent. This will make it easier to control his body.

GRIP AT THE ARMS

There are two basic distances at which you can come to grips with your opponent. First, there is the grip at the arms, which is typically shown with both wrestlers holding each other's arms near the elbow. There is also the grip at the body, which is either illustrated by the opponents having their hands clasped around each other's backs (sometimes called the "boy's grip" or the "peasant's grip") or by having one hand gripping the waist of the doublet and the other over the arm and gripping the shoulder.

While illustrated manuscripts show a variety of examples of these grips, all slightly different in their specifics, Ott provides us with clear and specific instruction on where and how to grip at both distances.

TECHNIQUE (vD 100v.1)

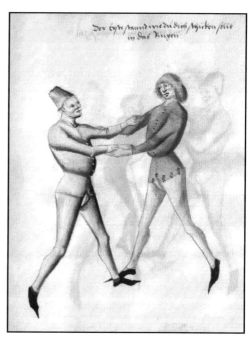

When you want to wrestle with an opponent by the arms, then be mindful always to grasp him with your left hand by his right bicep, and with your right hand grasp him outside his left arm. And with your left hand that you have on his bicep, press sharply backwards, and with the right hand grasp his left hand in front and pull it hard to you. And when you have seized him thus, then use whichever of the following described wrestling techniques you think best.

The Grip at the Arms shown in Paulus Kal, MS 1507, 81r

This grip at the arms is shown best by Paulus Kal in his section on wrestling.

1. Place yourself with your left leg leading and your hands before your thighs.

2. As you come to gripping distance, shift your weight slightly forwards and bring your hands up between his arms.

3. Grasp his right bicep, well above the elbow, with your left hand.

4. Grasp his left hand at the wrist with your right hand.

5. Push away with your left hand and pull with your right hand, which will open his body.

High and Low Stance

Coming to the grip from the inside

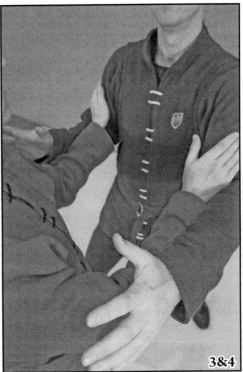

Neutral grip at the arms

KEY POINTS

- ❖ This will be the natural setup for anyone right-handed as it sets up throws utilizing the strength of the right side.

- ❖ The push-pull is key to setting up follow-on wrestling techniques.

- ❖ Execute the push-pull briskly.

- ❖ If he has gained grip on you, it's best to also get a hold of his arms in whatever manner you can to regain some control of the grip.

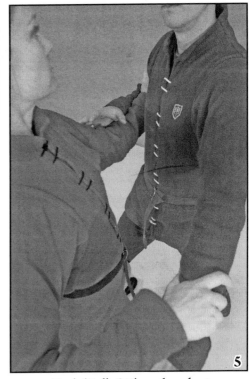

Push/Pull, Ott's preferred grip

The Grip at the Body in Talhoffer 1443 edition, 119v (Shows opposite side grip from Ott's description)

Neutral grip at the arms

GRIP AT THE BODY

The grip at the body can be done a variety of ways, but for the purpose of streamlining the instruction of techniques in the section on this grip, a very upright grip is used for the throws. This grip works very well for the larger of the opponents, as strength and size become increasingly important as you move closer to the body itself. There are a number of ways to escape this grip, however, so all is not lost for the smaller opponent. You can flow from a grip at the arms to a grip at the body, and this is described in a technique Ott recorded, as we show below.

TECHNIQUE (vD 106R.2)

> **Go through with your right hand, and grasp above the hip at his waist. And send your left hand above over his right shoulder, and grasp your right hand at the wrist and hold it fast....**

From the grip at the arms.

1. Drive your right arm under his left arm with a gathered step with your left foot to bring your body close to his.

2. Clasp his body tightly at the waist with your right hand.

3. Drive your left arm over his shoulder, clasping your right wrist and hold tight.

KEY POINTS

❖ Control his arms as you enter into this grip. Releasing both arms simultane-

Aron's right hand driving underneath

Grip at the Body

Alternate grip at the body

ously will give him an opening to counter your entry.

❖ He will likely mirror your grip at the body to regain some control of the clinch.

VARIATIONS

❖ You can also grip him with your right hand on the bottom of his doublet or on his belt and the left hand on the back of his right shoulder as shown in the Thott Talhoffer. He shows his body grips with a bent posture as opposed to the upright nature shown in the earlier 1443 Talhoffer and Kal's illustrations. Ott, however, doesn't specify this grip and therefore techniques at the body will require some alteration if this grip is used because of the bent posture of the wrestlers. Additionally when wrestlers fall into this position, their bodies tend to lock together. This alters the nature of the balance, making it much more reliant upon the opponent's pressure.

A variation of the Grip at the Body, in Talhoffer, MS Thott 290.2º, 52r

7

WRESTLING TECHNIQUES

As was discussed in Chapter 3, the organization of Ott's treatise leaves something to be desired for the modern practitioner wishes to work through and learn his wrestling techniques. The manual, particularly the second half, is without any discernible order and has such a large number of techniques; it is daunting material to work with.

In order to make sense of the disorganization of the second half of the manual, I have chosen to reorder the techniques thematically, and to somewhat condense them in order to make them more friendly for the modern practitioner to use in their training. This large number of techniques becomes even more manageable when we realize that some of the techniques are the same technique shown against a different entry and others are a counter to those that have come before.

After having done this, Ott's treatise can be summarized as:

> 2 Grips (shown in Chapter 6)
> 8 Techniques from Ott's grip
> 3 Techniques from the Wrist Lock
> 4 From a Chest Grip
> 16 From a Mutual Grip at the Arms
> 10 Techniques from a Mutual Grip at the Body
> 9 Techniques from Alternate Grips

This may seem somewhat a radical treatment of the manual, but I have found that the benefits gained by presenting a technique alongside it's counter far outweigh any potential negative that I have been able to foresee.

In light of the unorthodox treatment, I have made every effort to make it clear where in the original manual the techniques can be found. Each technique, as it is addressed, is presented with an index number that provides a clear reference point back to the original manual. Further, I have presented my interpretation along with the translation of the original techniques. Hopefully this transparency will allow anyone with an interest to reinterpret the techniques themselves.

Techniques from Ott's Grip

This set of techniques begin from the above mentioned biceps/wrist grip unless otherwise noted. This is Ott's preferred grip which gives an advantage in leverage and tactical options. The opponent will also have gained a grip against your arms in whatever way he can at that moment, despite the fact that it will be a suboptimal grip.

Techniques from the Wrist Lock

This set of techniques follow on from the opponent getting a strong grip on your arms. Initially the lock itself will be described and afterwards, throws that either follow after or counter the lock.

Techniques from a Chest Grip

This set of techniques follow on from the opponent getting a grip with both hands at your chest. Though this is an alternate grip, it is closely related to the techniques from the wrist lock and in fact could be considered interchangeable with them, hence the placement of these techniques immediately following the wrist lock.

Techniques from a Mutual Grip at the Arms

This set of techniques follow on from the opponent having a loose grip on your arms and you having a grip on him as well. This "mutual grip" is a mirrored grip where each person has their left hand inside on their opponent's right biceps and their right hand outside their opponent's left elbow.

TECHNIQUES FROM A MUTUAL GRIP AT THE BODY

This set of techniques follow on from the opponent having a grip on your body, where one arm of his is over your arm and his other is under your other arm. Typically this is performed as described earlier in Chapter 6, "Grip at the Body".

There are some varieties of grips at the body shown in Talhoffer which lead to other wrestling techniques that he shows, however it seems that all of Ott's techniques derive from this symmetrical over/under upright grip.

TECHNIQUES FROM ALTERNATE GRIPS

These sets of techniques are used to break free from grips to the collar, the body and the belt. There are many instances where you will not want to wrestle with an opponent at the body, most notably if he is significantly heavier or stronger than you are. Breaking free, then attempting to gain an advantageous grip might be the best tactical choice in this scenario.

UPWARD-BENT ELBOW ARM WRENCH

Ott's first technique is a wrench of the right shoulder, done by bending his arm and pulling it to yourself. It must be executed quickly and violently to be effective. It will cause him to react which sets up other techniques.

The First

When you have grasped him with your left hand at his right bicep and with the right hand in front by his left hand, then send your left hand out from his right arm, and grasp him below his right elbow and pull it to you. And with your right hand, with which you have his left hand, push his arm from you; thus you wrench his arm.

TECHNIQUE (vD 101R.1)

1. Beginning from the grip at the arms, take your left hand and slide it under your opponent's arm so that you are grabbing him underneath his forearm, fingers inside, thumb outside.

2. Pull his elbow past your own centerline towards your right shoulder, twisting it so that your left hand ends up facing the ceiling.

3. Push your opponent's left hand away and upwards, over his left shoulder to remove his center of balance and emphasize the wrenching isolation of the shoulder.

4. You can slide or step forwards with your left foot to place it behind his right foot, as shown in the "Upward Bent Rear Throw" on page 54.

TECHNIQUES FROM OTT'S GRIP

Push/Pull, Ott's preferred grip

Wrap of the right arm

Push of the left arm

KEY POINTS

❖ This is intended to be a wrench (joint lock) to the opponent's shoulder. As such, if using this technique in practice be aware of the potential for joint destruction and move slowly and carefully with your partner.

VARIATIONS

❖ A similar throw is shown in Fabian von Auerswald, "The Winding Away Over the Arm with One Hand" plates 11 & 12.

Maintain and strengthen pull

Pull of the left arm

THE SLIPPING THROUGH

The Slipping Through is a high-amplitude throw over the shoulders and back, similar to a fireman's carry. It seems to be a popular throw in German wrestling as it gets shown in many illustrated manuscripts.

> **Another**
>
> **Item: when you have seized him as before, then lift his left arm with your right hand, and send your head through the arm and pull it over your neck. And with your left hand grasp his left leg at the crook of his knee, and throw him thus over your back.**

TECHNIQUE (vD 101ʀ.2)

1. From Ott's preferred grip at the arms, pull your opponent's left arm towards you and upwards with your right hand, breaking his balance to his front-left opening.

2. Without releasing the pull on his arm, duck your head under his left arm at the shoulder so that your neck ends up in his armpit. Use bent knees and a slight forwards step with your left foot to your right to duck under.

3. Continue the pull on his arm, now directing it down to your chest or belly. This should optimally place his left shoulder over the right side of your neck, and should begin to load his upper body across your shoulders.

Duck the head

Pick up and dip right shoulder

4. Drive your left hand to his left knee, gripping him from the inside or outside (both are shown in various manuscripts).

5. Stand up quickly, scooping up his leg with your left hand, maintaining the pull downwards with your right hand, dip your right shoulder down, and raise your left arm, which will toss him over your back.

KEY POINTS

❖ Be sure that you are using an upright body to execute this throw. Do not bend over at the waist, as this will unbalance you to your toes.

❖ Be sure to pull his arm down to your chest with your right arm, not outwards to the right.

❖ Take care when performing this technique in practice as it results in a surprisingly high-amplitude throw.

VARIATIONS

❖ This throw is shown in many manuscripts including in Kal (*In Service of the Duke*, Tobler, page 182), Talhoffer (*Medieval Combat*, Rector, plate 196), and Auerswald's "Running through Under the Arm", plate 10.

COUNTER TO THE SLIPPING THROUGH

This counter employs a headlock on the opponent as he comes under the arm with his head. It requires good timing to properly employ.

Another Wrestling Technique

Item: when he intends to go through your arm with his head and throw you over his back, grasp him by the neck with the same arm and press him hard to you. And place your chest on him above, and push him down with your weight.

TECHNIQUE (vD 106v.5)

1. When your opponent has pulled your left arm over his neck, then clamp down tightly with your left arm under his neck.

2. Pull his head to your chest and hold strongly with your left arm.

3. Press him down to the ground by stepping back with your left leg and putting all of your weight onto him. This also removes your left leg out of his attempted grip.

KEY POINTS

❖ When executing this technique, turn your head to a side to avoid your chin or nose hitting his back if you hit the ground together.

❖ You can slip your legs back into a sprawl to drive him to the ground.

❖ The right arm can be brought in to clasp your left hand to tighten the grip even more.

❖ Use caution when executing this technique as it can wrench the neck violently.

VARIATIONS

❖ This counter is shown in many manuscripts including in Kal (*In Service of the Duke*, Tobler, page 183), and Talhoffer (*Medieval Combat*, Rector, plate 197). Talhoffer shows an additional counter on plate 197, not described in Ott, which involves grabbing around the armpit of the opponent, pivoting forward with the right leg and grasping between the opponent's legs with the right hand.

TECHNIQUES FROM OTT'S GRIP

The opponent pulls your arm over his neck

Clamp the neck hand

Press down with your weight

Push/Pull, Ott's preferred grip

UPWARD-BENT ELBOW REAR THROW

This throw is the same as the "Upward-bent elbow arm wrench" already described on page 41, but with the addition of a springing step behind the opponent's leg to throw him to his back.

Another Wrestling from the First Hold

Item: lift his left arm with your right hand and grasp him with your left hand under to his elbow and pull it to you. And with your right hand, push his arm away from you above, and spring with your left foot behind his right to throw him off his feet over your left leg.

TECHNIQUE (vD 101r.3)

1. Beginning from Ott's preferred grip at the arms, lift your opponent's left arm with your right arm as though you will be throwing him with the Slipping Through. This will make him pull backwards in resistance to the forwards throw.

2. Twist your left hand around his arm so that you are grabbing him underneath his forearm, fingers inside, thumb outside.

3. Pull his right elbow past your own centerline. This should put pressure on his shoulder and begin to turn his body counter-clockwise as he attempts to relieve the pressure. This also begins to break his balance.

Wrap of the right arm

4. Push his left hand away above his left shoulder. This will continue breaking his balance and make it impossible for him to fight effectively against the shoulder wrench.

5. Spring vigorously behind his right foot with your left foot and throw him backwards over your left leg.

KEY POINTS

❖ Make sure you move your left hand to his forearm, just below his elbow, that is, to the meat of the forearm just to the hand-side of the elbow.

❖ As you step in, assure that you increase the pressure on his shoulder, not release it. This will make him put his own weight backwards, breaking his balance and enabling the throw.

VARIATIONS

❖ A similar throw is shown in Fabian von Auerswald, "The Winding Away Over the Arm with One Hand" plates 11 & 12.

Push of the left arm

The finish from the other side

Push/Pull, Ott's preferred grip

TURNING THROUGH

This throw is done by isolating his right arm and either pulling him to your left or right with both hands to throw him to the ground.

Another Wrestling from the First Hold

Item: hold his right hand fast with your left hand and grasp with your left hand to help your right. And hold his arm fast with both hands, and turn yourself through his arm to his right side; thus you overwhelm him from behind; or turn yourself through to your left side.

TECHNIQUE (vD 101v.1)

1. From Ott's preferred grip at the arms, slip your left hand down his arm to grasp his right hand strongly with your left, and then release his wrist with your right hand and grasp his right arm just above your left hand.

2. Pull his arm strongly forwards and across to your right side waist as you pass backwards with your right foot.

3. As you pass back, drive your left shoulder into the back of his upper arm at the shoulder joint. This will throw him down onto his front.

KEY POINTS

❖ Do not release the pulling pressure on him as you step, but ensure you maintain the broken balance.

Slip the left hand to the wrist

Grasp with right hand and turn in

TURNING THROUGH (CONTINUED)

VARIATIONS

❖ Ott describes two turning options in this one technique. One can either pass away with your right foot "turning yourself through to your left side" or by stepping in with your right foot, "turning through to his right side."

Another (vD 101v.2)

Item: hold his left hand fast with both hands and turn yourself through his arm to his left side, and pull his left arm over your right shoulder and break downwards.

Grasp with the right hand and turn in

Completion

❖ The turning through can also create an arm-break by gripping both hands on his left arm, and passing backwards with your left foot, turning away and pulling his arm over your right shoulder and breaking downwards.

❖ NOTE: It is extremely easy to deliver a debilitating injury your opponent with this technique. It should be practiced ONLY with great care.

Counter the Turning Through thus: (vD 101v.3)

Item: when an opponent goes through you, then also go through, and fall to whichever of these wrestling techniques you wish.

❖ The Turning Through can also be used to counter itself. As your opponent begins to turn through you, you can use footwork to circle opposite of his movement as he enters, resetting you both to a neutral position relative to one another. It is telling that in this counter Ott tells us to "fall to whichever of the wrestling techniques" we desire. This clarifies that the counter isn't a throw, but that we have simply nullified our opponent's attack.

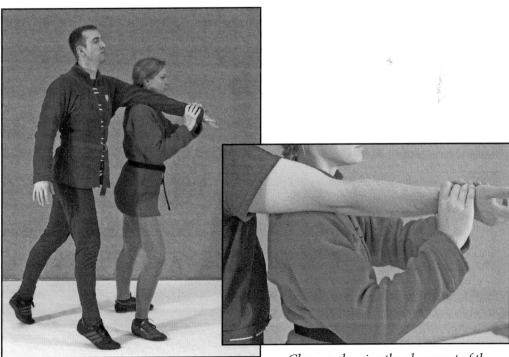

Arm break variation

Close up showing the placement of the upper arm against gthe shoulder joint

Push/Pull, Ott's preferred grip

REAR HIP THROW

This technique's entry is related to the turning through, but rather than enabling a forward throw, you set him up with your pull to resist backwards and take him off his feet that way.

> **Another Wrestling Technique**
>
> **Grasp his right [33] hand with both hands and jerk him to your right side. And step with your right foot behind his right foot, and send your right arm to his left side and throw him over your right hip.**

TECHNIQUE (vD 106r.3)

1. Grasp his right hand with both hands and pull him strongly to your right. This off-balancing should cause him to step slightly in that direction with his right foot.

2. Step with your right foot behind his right foot and simultaneously send your right hand across his front to his left side.

3. Throw him before yourself over your right hip.

---

[33] In Ringeck, the left hand is pulled, making for a very awkward and seemingly impractical technique. In light of this, it is likely that the variation between Von Danzig and Ringeck is due to a scribal error.

Pull right to right side

Stepping through

KEY POINTS

❖ This can be done as a feint, meaning that you can search for either this technique or the Turning Through and react *Indes* to choose the superior response, depending on his momentum.

❖ This throw can deposit your opponent on his head, so beware in practice.

VARIATIONS

❖ A similar throw is shown in Fabian von Auerswald, "The Two Hips" plate 26.

Jess slips her left hand to the wrist   *Aron drives the left hand in*

REAR THROW AT THE WAIST

To counter the Bent-Elbow Wrench, Downward-Bent Elbow Throw, Slipping Through, Turning Through, or Stepping Behind. This technique is shown on the opposite side than is written, so as to maintain continuity with the previously shown throws.

Note that this technique counters all the wrestling from the first stance

Item: this is for when he has grasped your left hand with his right and intends to grasp through below onto your elbow with his left hand, intending to wrench your arm or to come to help his right hand and turn himself through your arm. Then note when he grasps with the left to help the right or grasps for your elbow, and simultaneously send your right arm over his left at his right side, seizing him by the waist. Spring with your right foot behind his left, and throw him off his feet over your right leg.

Another Wrestling Technique

If he grasps your left hand with both hands and wants to pull you to his right side, then send your right hand through from above over his left arm. And with this, send your right hand to grasp his right side, and with your left, fall to the crook of one of his knees.

TECHNIQUE (vD 101v.4, vD 105r.2)

1. When your opponent grasps for your right hand with his left, then drive your lecft hand to his left side, pinning his right arm down.

Step behind and throw　　　　　　　*Completion*

2. As you step behind his right leg with your left leg, clasp his waist at his left side with an inverted left hand, your elbow pointed upwards, pulling his body tight against yours. This will drive him off-balance to his back.

3. Leverage him backwards with your elbow by maintaining a hold on him with your hand but driving down and back with the elbow to throw him off his feet.

VARIATIONS

❖ This throw can also be done by grabbing his right leg with your right arm, enabling a very powerful throw, shown in 105r.2.

KEY POINTS

❖ This counter must be done before he begins to pull you to your right.

❖ Counter IMMEDIATELY with his release of your left arm.

VARIATION

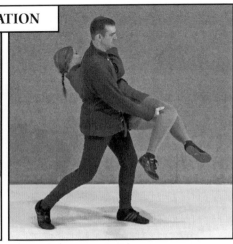

Grasping to the leg with the right arm　　　　　　　*Throwing*

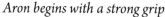

Aron begins with a strong grip   *Jess enacts wrist lock*

WRIST LOCK AT THE CHEST

The Wrist Lock at the Chest is a very useful technique to counter a strong grip. It works well if he has grabbed your arm or if he has gotten a hold of your jacket at the chest. This technique negates the strength advantage by attacking one of the weakest points of the opponent's body with both arms, doubling your strength, and provides a fantastic opening to a number of throws, which follow from this technique. It could also lead him to release his grip, allowing you to escape.

Another wrestling technique

Item: if he grasps your arms above with strength, and holds you fast and wants to press you, then send your right arm outside over his left in front by his hand, and grasp your right hand with your left hand. And press his hand with both of your hands toward your chest.

TECHNIQUE (vD 102r.1)

1. The opponent has grabbed your arms on the biceps or upper arms and is using his strength and superior grip to move you around.

2. Drive your right arm over his left, maintaining a straight wrist by driving your outer wrist bone into the bones of his wrist.

3. Bring your left hand to hold your own right hand, and with both hands press his left forearm or hand tightly into your chest.

Completion

Closeup of completion, showing position of wrist bones on Aron's hand/wrist

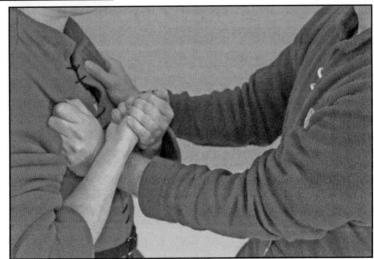

KEY POINTS

❖ When you apply this wrist lock, be sure that your right hand is positioned against your own chest as though you were pressing the bottom of your fist against your chest.

❖ Do not fold your right wrist, this will allow for space in the lock and he will be able to pull from it.

VARIATIONS

❖ Step back with your forward foot slightly and bend your knees. This will apply greater pain on the lock and may bring your opponent to his knees.

❖ A similar throw is shown in Fabian von Auerswald, "The Weakening of the Arms", plate 7.

SHOULDER-KNEE REAR THROW

This throw is a basic rear throw of a kind that we see frequently throughout German wrestling, powered by pressing the upper body with one arm and pulling the lower body with the other. In this case it is shown against a grip at the chest or after you have completed the "Wrist Lock at the Chest."

> **Note: if he has his hand at your chest, then spring with your right foot behind his left, and grasp with your left hand to the crook of his left knee. And lift with that, and with your right hand push him above away from you; thus he will fall.**

TECHNIQUE (vD 102r.2)

1. Put your opponent into the wristlock just taught, then spring with your right foot outside behind his left foot.

2. Grab his left knee with your left hand and yank it upwards toward your left armpit, keeping it close to your body.

3. At the same time, reach across his upper body with your right hand and push it away above.

KEY POINTS

❖ This technique is easily done if, when you get the wrist lock on your opponent, he attempts to pull back and away from you. You can then follow him *Indes* into this rear throw.

❖ We are told to lift his leg before putting pressure above. This will prevent him from stepping backwards as you step into him and release the pressure of the wrist lock.

❖ Note that the technique says "if he has his hand is at your chest" implying that this throw is possible whenever he grabs to your chest.

VARIATIONS

❖ A similar throw is shown in Fabian von Auerswald, "The Weakening of the Arms", plate 7, though Auerswald has us strip the opponent's left arm across his body providing a large upper opening to exploit before stepping in for the throw.

Wrist lock from new angle

Spring and push

ELBOW TO THE BALANCE

This technique is referred to as "Elbow to the Balance" in many treatises, and is shown numerous times from a variety of entries. Whenever his left hand is open and loosely gripping, or in the case of this wrist lock not gripping at all, you can execute this technique.

Another

Note: when you are pressing his hand in front to your chest with both of your hands, and he has his hand open and extends his fingers, then grasp him by the fingers with your left hand and lift upwards to your left side. And with your right hand, take him off balance by the elbow.

start & 1

Wrist lock from new angle

TECHNIQUE (vD 102r.3)

1. Beginning again from the wrist lock, this time you feel that his hand is open against your chest.

2. Grasp the outside of his left hand with your left hand. This is done best if you can grab his pinky and ring finger along with some meat of the hand.

3. Pull his hand away from your chest and lift it upwards and to your left side. This should create a wrist lock and point his elbow upwards, as well as to break his balance to his front balance point.

4. With your right hand, drive his elbow to your left side.

KEY POINTS

❖ Be sure when you are grasping for his hand with your left that you do not release the wrist lock with your right until you have secured his small fingers. Keep the pressure towards your own chest until you are sure of your grip and then explosively move to the throw.

❖ When pulling his hand upwards and to your left, keep the movement close to your body so as to keep the pressure on the joints.

VARIATIONS

❖ This is shown in many manuscripts including in Kal (*In Service of the Duke*, Tobler, page 192), who illustrates that you can step in front of him with your right leg, creating a barrier for his left leg.

TECHNIQUES FROM A WRIST LOCK

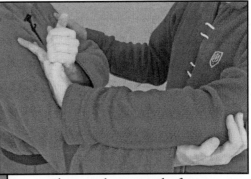

Closeup of gripping the fingers

2&3

Pulling hand up and over

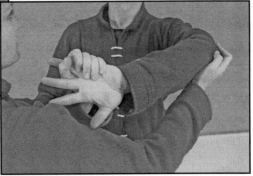

Pulling hand away, gripping the elbow

4

Pushing elbow to left side

Closeup of grip on the elbow

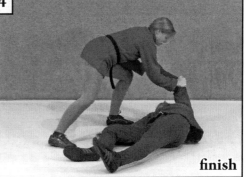

finish

Aron has grabbed Jess at the chest

STRAIGHT-ARM THROW

The Straight-Arm Throw is used when the opponent grips you at the chest with both hands. It is a simple technique, trapping his hands in place once he grabs you and following with a hard press to his elbow, which could lead to a lock, a throw or a break. The version Ott describes is a throw, shown below.

Another Wrestling Technique

If he seizes you in front by the chest with both hands, then send your right hand above over his left and control it, and send your left hand onto his right elbow. And create a barrier with your left foot.[34]

TECHNIQUE (vD 105r.3)

1. Your opponent has grabbed you in front of your chest with both hands. The outsides of the chest, almost in front of the shoulders where the sleeves meet the body of a jacket is where there would have been looser material making for an easy grip on a medieval doublet.

2. Drive your right hand over his left wrist and contain it, grabbing his right hand at your chest.

---

[34] The Ringeck manuscript advises to use the right foot, which seems less practical, but which can be done.

Reach across both wrists

Push his elbow

Another angle

3. Drive your left hand onto his right elbow and push it to your right, as though you were driving it over his left arm.

4. As you push, step with your left foot to the inside of his right foot and throw him off his feet over your leg.

KEY POINTS

❖ This throw can affect a straight-arm bar and can therefore easily break your opponent's arm. Use caution when performing this throw in practice.

VARIATIONS

❖ If his right arm happens to be bent when you perform this throw, it can also be done as the Elbow to the Balance, as detailed above.

Aron has grabbed Jess at the chest   *Pushing arm up and across*

FORWARD HIP THROW

This technique is shown numerous times with different entries. It is a basic hip throw, common to many martial arts and is represented in many illustrated texts. This technique is shown on the opposite side than is written, so as to maintain continuity with the previously shown throws.

> **Item: if he holds you with both hands in front of your chest, then push his right elbow up, and turn yourself through and grasp him at the waist.**

TECHNIQUE (vD 107r.5)

1. Your opponent has gripped you in front of your chest with both hands.

2. Grip his left triceps with your right hand. Drive your right hand onto his left elbow, pushing it upwards and to the left. This will momentarily break his grip on you, and provide an opening for you to attack, as well as breaking his balance to his front right opening.

3. Turn your body into him, stepping with both of your feet before his feet, and grasp around behind him to his waist with your right arm. Clasp his body tightly onto your body, further breaking his balance.

4. Throw him before you over your hip, by rotating to the left and pulling him over your hip with your right arm.

Stepping and reaching around

Pulling over hip

KEY POINTS

❖ DO NOT bend at the waist to throw him, rather bend your knees to get your center of balance below his, and use the straightening of your legs to propel him upwards and forwards, pulling strongly with your left hand on his right arm to throw him around your body.

❖ Step in closely to his body. The closer you are, the easier this throw is to accomplish.

❖ When you put your hand around behind his waist, clasp him tightly to you which will pull him to his front-center balance point.

❖ Do not run into him as your step in, as this will send his balance backwards and make the throw harder to accomplish.

VARIATIONS

❖ A similar throw is shown in Talhoffer, (*Medieval Combat*, Rector) plate 194, though a slight variation is shown where the thrower has his left arm over and across the shoulders rather than clasping the waist. This is a common variation to use if the thrower is taller than the man being hip-thrown.

Jess begins the wrist lock

ELBOW-STRIKE REAR THROW

This technique is used to counter whenever you cannot move your arm. Here, it counters against the Wrist Lock at the Chest.

Another Wrestling Technique

When you have grasped his right bicep with your left hand and you press him backward with it, and he falls with his right arm from outside over your left hand, and presses your hand fast to his chest, then send the same elbow to his right side and sink down. And spring with your left foot behind his right, and grasp with your right hand to the crook of his knee, and throw him down before you.

TECHNIQUE (vD 107r.6)

1. Your opponent has fallen over your left hand with his right to execute the wrist lock against you

2. Strike his right side with your left elbow, sinking down low and springing in with the left foot to power the strike. You should get your left foot behind his right foot with this step and strike. This strike should be hard enough to knock the wind out of him and to rock him back on his heels slightly.

Aron strikes and steps

Pick up leg and throw

3. Grab his right knee with your right hand, and lift it up to your chest

4. At the same time, push with the hand that is on his chest so that he falls onto his back.

KEY POINTS

❖ When you drive in with the same-side elbow as the locked wrist; this releases the pressure of the lock and frees you somewhat from it.

❖ This can be a powerful strike to the ribs and can knock his breath out of him, especially when you sink down with the strike. This gives you an *Indes* moment to exploit as he is momentarily stunned.

❖ The strike should get his momentum moving backwards, making this throw easier to execute.

Mutual grip

ELBOW TO THE BALANCE

This throw is shown numerous times from a variety of entries, and has already been shown from a grip at the chest after the Wrist Lock at the Chest on page 68. The only difference in this version is that it begins from the Mutual Grip.

Another Wrestling Technique

When you want to wrestle with an opponent and he holds you loosely at the arms, then grasp with your left hand above over his right, and grasp his left hand by the fingers or otherwise, and lift towards your left. And with your right hand take him off balance by his elbow.

TECHNIQUE (vD 102r.4)

1. Your opponent has you by the arms loosely, drive your left hand over his right and grasp to his left hand.

2. Grasp the outside of his left hand with your left hand. This is done best if you can grab his pinky and ring finger along with the meat of his hand.

3. Pull his hand away from your arm and lift it upwards and to your left side. This should create a wrist lock and point his elbow upwards.

4. With your right hand, drive his elbow to your left, into his front right balance point.

Grasping the hand

Pulling the hand away

KEY POINTS

❖ When pulling his hand upwards and to your left, keep the movement close to your body so as to keep the pressure on the joints.

VARIATIONS

❖ This is shown in many manuscripts including in Kal (*In Service of the Duke*, Tobler, page 192), who illustrates that you can step in front of him with your right leg, creating a barrier for his left leg.

Grasping the hand

FORWARD HIP THROW

There are three different counters shown for the Elbow to the Balance. They seem to have distinct applications depending on how late into the moment of *Indes* you reply to the Elbow to the Balance. The initial opening presented with the Elbow to the Balance when the opponent reac hes across, commmitting both armns to one side of their body. Here we see the Forward Hip Throw exploiting this opening in its application as a counter against Elbow to the Balance.

Counter that thus

When someone does this, and grasps with his left hand to your fingers and wants to unbalance you with the right, then send your right hand under his left arm around the body. And spring with your right foot before both of his feet, and throw him thus over your right hip.

TECHNIQUE (vD 102v.1)

1. Your opponent grabs your left hand with his left and intends to unbalance you with his right hand on your elbow.

2. As soon has he has removed his left arm from you and provided an opening on the left side of his body, turn your body into him, stepping across with your rightfoot past both of his feet, and grasp around behind him to his waist with your right hand. Make sure your hips are below his hips as you come in low and with flexed knees.

Reaching around

Pulling over the hip

3. At the same time as you turn into him, grip his right arm at the bicep with your left hand if you hadn't already done so with the mutual grip and pull it hard down and towards your hip.

4. Throw him before you over your right hip by straightening your legs and rotating your body, pulling hard with the left arm.

KEY POINTS

❖ The opening will be created for you to enter when he reaches with his left hand to grasp your left hand.

❖ DO NOT bend at the waist to throw him, rather bend your knees to get your center of balance below yours, and use the straightening of your legs to propel him upwards and forwards, pulling strongly with your right hand on his left arm to throw him around your body.

❖ Step in closely to his body. The closer you are, the easier this throw is to accomplish.

❖ When you put your hand around behind his waist, clasp him tightly to you which will pull him to his front-center balance point.

Grasping the hand

ELBOW-STRIKE REAR THROW

As the second counter for Elbow to the Balance, this technique is used when he grasps your hand, for as we have seen in the Wrist Lock at the Chest on page 64, the technique counters when you cannot withdraw your hand.

> **Or Counter it thus**
>
> **When he has grasped your left hand with his left hand and wants to unbalance you with his right hand, then sink down, and go to him with your left elbow to his waist. Spring with your left foot behind his right foot, grasp his right leg with your right hand at the crook of his knee, and pull toward you. With the left push him away from you above; thus he will fall.**

TECHNIQUE (vD 102v.2)

1. Your opponent grabs your left hand with his left and intends to unbalance you with his right hand on your elbow and has removed your hand from his bicep and is holding your hand but has not yet drawn it across his body.

2. Strike his right side with your left elbow, sinking down low and springing in with the left foot to power the strike. You should get your left foot behind his right foot with this step and strike. This strike should be hard enough to knock the wind out of him and to rock him back on his heels slightly.

Striking with the elbow

Reach across and grab knee

3. Grab his right knee with your right hand, and lift it up to your chest

4. At the same time, drive your left hand across his chest so that he falls onto his back.

KEY POINTS

❖ When you drive in with the same-side elbow as the grabbed hand, this releases the power of his pull to your right and frees you somewhat from it. If he has begun to get his hand in place on your left elbow, you can free it with your sinking low and striking against him.

❖ This can be a powerful strike to the ribs and can knock his breath out of him especially when you sink down with it. This gives you a moment to exploit.

❖ The strike should get his momentum moving backwards, making this throw easier to execute.

REAR HIP THROW

The third counter for the Elbow to the Balance, the Rear Hip Throw is your last opportunity to clearly counter the Elbow to the Balance. In this case your opponent has now committed both hands to his left side, providing an opening on his right. This technique has been shown on page 56 as a combination technique to the Turning Through.

Another

Note: when he grasps your left hand with his left hand, and tries to unbalance you with his right and pushes your left elbow up in the air, then turn your head through and send your right arm to his left flank; and spring with your right foot behind his right foot, and throw him over your right hip. Or grasp one of his legs with your right hand as you turn through, and jerk him toward you.

TECHNIQUE (vD 102v.3)

1. Your opponent grabs your left hand with his left and intends to unbalance you with his right hand on your elbow and has removed your hand from his bicep and has begun to push your left elbow into the air.

2. Drive through with your head under your own left arm and step with your right foot behind his right foot and simultaneously send your right hand across his front to his left side.Throw him before yourself over your right hip.

KEY POINTS

❖ This throw may deposit your opponent on his head, so beware in practice.

VARIATIONS

❖ A similar throw is shown in Fabian von Auerswald, "The Two Hips" plate 26.

❖ When you turn through under your arm, step less deeply and grasp his right leg with your right arm and jerk it upwards to your chest. This will throw him backwards onto his back.

TECHNIQUES FROM A MUTUAL GRIP AT THE ARMS

Jess lifts Aron's arm

*Perspective shift
to the other side
for clarity*

Aron ducks his head and steps

finish

Mutual grip

UPWARD-BENT ELBOW REAR THROW

This throw is enacted by pushing the opponent's arm backward over his head, causing him to fall over your leg.

> **Another Wrestling Technique**
>
> **Strike out his left hand with your right hand, and grasp the fingers of his right hand. Grasp his right arm which you struck upwards in front with your left hand, and throw him backwards over your left leg.**

TECHNIQUE (vD 104v.2)

1. Your opponent holds you loosely in the mutual grip at the arms.

2. Strike out his left hand with your right hand.

3. Grab the fingers of his right hand from your arm. Pull them away and over his head. Continue that motion with your left hand against his elbow, pushing it to his rear.

4. Step behind his right foot with your left foot and throw him to his back before you.

Strike out arm

Grab right arm and push back

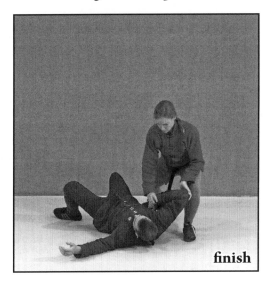

KEY POINTS

❖ The arm must be pushed backwards forcefully with your step to unbalance him to his back.

VARIATIONS

❖ Because of the ambiguity of Ott's text, another possibility is that you push his right arm over the left side of his head, and step behind his left leg with your left leg. This creates a cross-body pressure which will make him trip backwards over your left leg.

Mutual grip

Grab and pull arm

INVERTED THROW

This technique begins with a setup that looks and feels like the Elbow to the Balance but instead turns into a rear throw. It is quite powerful and could easily deposit your opponent on his head.

> **Another Wrestling Technique**
>
> **If he holds you loosely by the arms, then grasp with your left hand to his right, and grasp him by the fingers. And hold him fast and strike up with your right hand, and go through under his right arm, and grasp him by the flank, and with your left hand at the crook of his knee.**

TECHNIQUE (vD 105v.5)

1. Your opponent holds you loosely in the mutual grip at the arms.

2. Strike free from his grip with your left hand and by striking down on his arm and grab the fingers of his right hand with your left and hold him tightly.

3. Strike up his left hand with your right hand and drive your head, body and right arm underneath his right arm.

4. Send your right hand around behind his back and clasp him tightly around the waist.

5. Grab his left knee with your left hand and stand, dropping him on his head.

TECHNIQUES FROM A MUTUAL GRIP AT THE ARMS

Drive body in

Lift leg and stand

KEY POINTS

❖ This throw will deposit your opponent on his head, so beware in practice.

VARIATIONS

❖ A similar throw is shown in Talhoffer (*Medieval Combat*, Rector), plate 201.

Mutual grip

DOUBLE LEG PICKUP

This is a common throw across many styles of wrestling, where you shoot in and pick up both knees of the opponent, dropping him to his back and having control of his legs.

Another Wrestling Technique

Strike out with both hands and fall to the crooks of both of his knees and pull them to you. And push him above with your head to his chest; thus he will fall.

TECHNIQUE (vD 105v.2)

1. Your opponent holds you loosely in the mutual grip at the arms.

2. Strike out both hands from the inside.

3. Drive both hands to his knees and your head to his chest with a step in with either foot, bending deeply at the knees to enable the grab.

4. Stand, lifting his knees to your armpits while simultaneously pushing on his chest with the top of your head.

KEY POINTS

❖ This throw is commonly used in modern wrestling, and can be highly effective if done with surprise.

Striking out the arms

Grab both knees, drive head into chest

Pull knees up, throw man

Jess grabs Aron's knees

SPRAWLING COUNTER

This technique counters the Double Leg Pickup Throw by getting a headlock on him as he enters and sprawling back with your feet, driving him to the ground. We have seen a similar action in the counter to the Slipping Through on page 52.

Counter This Thus

Grasp him above by the neck under his armpits, and place yourself right on him above. And step well back with your feet, so that he cannot grasp either one; thus you press him to the ground.

TECHNIQUE (vD 105v.3)

1. Your opponent shoots in and grabs both knees, putting his head against your chest.

2. Immediately drive both of your hands around his neck (or as shown here for safety, around his chest), outside of both of his arms, and place your chest on top of his head.

3. Step back quickly with both feet at the same time so that his hands are pulled away from your knees.

4. Put all of your weight into your chest and drive him to the ground.

Aron grabs under Jess's neck

KEY POINTS

❖ When you perform this counter be sure that you turn your head to one side or the other so that you don't drive your own chin into his back.

❖ You will both fall quickly, and this could be fairly punishing to your partner so take consideration as to your relative sizes before dropping violently on him in practice.

Step back and sprawl

VARIATIONS

❖ A similar counter is shown in Talhoffer (*Medieval Combat*, Rector), plate 209.

All weight on the upper back

Jess grabs for Aron's doublet

GROIN LIFTING THROW

This throw is surprisingly effective and can send a smaller opponent flying with the force between the lower hand pulling and the upper hand pushing away.

Another Wrestling Technique

Strike out his left with your right hand, and send your right in front between his legs, seizing him behind by the doublet or on the arm. And lift him thus and push him away from you above with your left hand; thus he will fall backwards onto his head.

TECHNIQUE (vD 104v.3)

1. Your opponent holds you loosely in the mutual grip at the arms.

2. Strike out his left hand with your right

3. Drive your right hand between his legs with a deep lunge in with your right foot and grab him behind on the jacket or belt.

4. Quickly stand, pushing him away, upwards and backwards, at the neck with your left hand.

TECHNIQUES FROM A MUTUAL GRIP AT THE ARMS

Aron grabs for the elbow

Drive hand between legs and grab doublet

KEY POINTS

❖ This throw is surprisingly effective and with modification (below) does not rely upon medieval clothing. Other modification possibilities are grabbling the opponent's belt, belt loop or pants waist.

❖ This throw will deposit your opponent on his head, so beware in practice.

VARIATIONS

❖ When entering for the throw, rather than releasing his right hand, you can drive it behind him with your left hand and grab it with your own right hand. You can then stand up quickly and lift him with your right hand and push against his throat to throw him backwards onto his head.

COUNTER TO THE GROIN LIFTING THROW

Here we see yet another counter that works by employing encircling a low attack with both hands. In this case, you are encircling the arm and possibly breaking the opponent's elbow.

> **Counter This Thus**
>
> **When he sends his right hand through between your legs and seizes you behind by the doublet, then bend your head against him, and send both your arms through from the outside below his right arm, and lift upwards with it. Thus he cannot throw you.**

TECHNIQUE (vD 104v.4)

1. Your opponent strikes out your left arm and drives his right hand between your legs to throw you.

2. Bend your head forwards and drive both hands around his arm, and lift his arm upwards.

KEY POINTS

❖ Bending your head forwards is a big part of the reason this works. Your opponent will be trying to throw you backwards and will succeed if you do not counter that action.

❖ Clamping your thighs together as you perform this technique will prevent you from pulling your opponent's arm into your groin.

Jess drives her hand between legs

Aron grabs Jess under her elbow

COUNTER TO A BAR

Despite the sometimes ambiguous language of many of medieval techniques, this is by far the most unclear in Ott's treatise. I have interpreted the "bar" as a grip over the hand.

A Counter to a Bar

When he tries to use a bar with his right hand, then bar with your left.

TECHNIQUE (vD 105v.1)

1. Your opponent reaches over your hands with his right hand to enable a throw (as in the "Straight Arm Throw.")

2. Pull your left hand out from below, and use it to push against his right arm, blocking it into place, and stepping behind him with your left foot, throw him off his feet and onto his back.

KEY POINTS

❖ It is important that you move *Indes* and counter him as his right arm is coming across. If you wait until he has clamped your hands tightly to his chest this technique will not work.

NOTE

This technique is exceedingly ambiguous. It's location within the text gives no clues as to it's context. However, the word here translated as "bar" has the additional implications of a "fence" or "blockade". After looking through techniques in Ott's treatise that call for one to "fence in" with the right hand, this seems to be a likely interpretation.

TECHNIQUES FROM A MUTUAL GRIP AT THE ARMS

Reaching across forming a "bar"

Counter by "barring" with left

Mutual grip

SAME-SIDE REAR THROW

This throw is similar to the Shoulder Knee Rear Throw we have already learned where the left knee is picked up by the left hand, except for in this case the throw is being performed by attacking the left knee with the right hand.

Another Wrestling Technique

Item: when you have each grasped each other by the arms and he holds you loosely, then strike out his left arm down from above with your right hand. And grasp him with it in the crook of his left knee, and pull toward you and push in front on the left side of his chest with your left hand. Thus he must fall.

TECHNIQUE (vD 103r.1)

1. You and your opponent are holding each other in the mutual grip at the arms and he holds you loosely.

2. Strike his left arm out by going from the outside to the inside and drive your hand down to his left knee.

3. Grasp his left knee and pull it towards your right armpit and push to your right with your left hand to his left shoulder.

Reaching across

Pick up

KEY POINTS

❖ It is important that you not lift his knee, but pull his knee to your own side, which will drag him off-balance to your left side, spiraling him downwards.

finish

ELBOW TO THE BALANCE

Here we see Elbow to the Balance again, this time being used as a counter against a rear throw. There is also a subtlety to the way it is written, which lets us know we can perform this technique not just as a counter, but whenever he grasps our chest with his hand.

Counter that thus

Note: when he grasps to your chest in front with his left hand, then grasp his left hand with your left, and take him off balance by his elbow with your right hand. Or push his elbow out with your right hand, straight upwards, and thus turn him away from you.

TECHNIQUE (vD 103R.2)

1. Your opponent grasps to your chest with his left hand, then grasp his left hand with your left.

2. Grasp the outside of his left hand with your left hand. This is done best if you can grab his pinky and ring finger along with some meat of the hand.

3. Pull his hand away from your chest and lift it upwards and to your left side. This should create a wrist lock and point his elbow upwards, as well as to break his balance to his front balance point.

4. With your right hand, drive his elbow to your left side.

Reaching across

Elbow to the balance

VARIATIONS

❖ When your opponent grasps to your chest with his left hand, you can drive your right hand to his elbow, pushing it away straight upwards, which will turn him away from you.

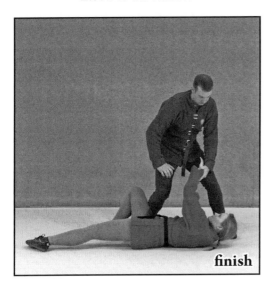

Mutual grip *Reaching across*

OPENING THROW

Similar in nature to the "Inverted Throw", this throw is best to be performed on a smaller opponent.

Another Wrestling Technique

When you each have each other by the arms and he holds you loosely, then strike his right hand out with your left hand downwards from above, and send it through below his right arm and grasp him behind. And hold him fast and pull towards you, and with your right hand grasp him outside to the crook of his right knee. Thus you throw him to the left side. This works on both sides.

TECHNIQUE (vD 103ʀ.3)

1. When you are holding each other by the arms and he holds you loosely

2. Strike his right hand with your left hand, downwards from above, by sending your hand outside and over his. Then shoot your hand under his armpit.

3. Continue the movement of your left hand under his right arm, and drive through his arm and around to be behind his left-side waist.

4. Pull him towards you with your left arm, and bend your knees, grabbing his right knee from the outside with your right hand.

5. Stand, and he will fall to his left side.

Grasping knee

Lift

KEY POINTS

❖ Do not bend over at the waist when entering this throw, or you open yourself up to be countered. Bend at the knees.

Mutual grip

FOOT STRIKE REAR THROW

This throw is quite interesting as it is rare in the German lexicon of wrestling techniques to do what appears to be a footsweep to the ankle. It is extremely effective when paired with the hand to the throat.

Another Wrestling Technique

If he has his right foot forward, then pull his right hand with your left, and strike him with the left foot down to his right ankle. And thus jerk him down. Or fall with the right hand to his throat as you strike out his foot, and push him over backward.

TECHNIQUE (vD 105v.4)

1. When you are holding each other by the arms and he has his right foot forwards

2. Strike down and across with your left foot onto his right ankle

3. Pull strongly down and toward you on his right arm with your left hand to jerk him down, while pushing away with your right hand on his left arm.

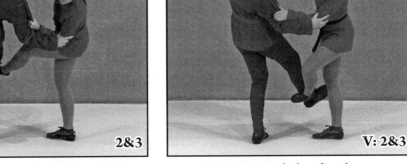

Striking the foot

Variation: right hand to throat

KEY POINTS

❖ Do not let up on the pull when you strike down with your own foot. You may strike his foot out from under him, but it's not necessary for the throw.

❖ Your right hand should also keep the pressure on him to your left to assist the throw.

VARIATIONS

❖ You can strike him in the throat with your right hand to throw him over as you strike out his foot. This is a good modification if paired with someone who is stronger.

❖ You can also pull him over a planted right foot by pulling hard down and to your left side with your left arm while pulling hard up and to your left side with your right arm. This will trip him over his planted foot, rather than striking it out as shown.

COUNTER TO THE FOOT STRIKE REAR THROW

This counter could be for the previous foot strike, which is how I have chosen to interpret it (by presenting it from the opposite side of Ott's example), though it could just as easily apply to a variety of throws where you are being pulled over an ankle crossing.

> **A Counter to the Bar**
>
> **Note: when you each have grasped each other by the arms and you have your left foot forward, and he is then cunning and steps with his right foot outside behind your left and wants to jerk you over it by the arms, then quickly pull your left foot back. And with this, seize his right foot and push him above at the chest; thus he will fall.**

TECHNIQUE (vD 104r.4)

1. If your opponent wants to jerk you over the foot by your arms, then quickly step back with your left foot

2. Seize his left foot with your right hand, and pressing him with your left hand on his chest, throw him backwards to the ground.

KEY POINTS

❖ You must be very quick to catch his foot while it's still in the air after missing your own.

VARIATIONS

❖ If the foot catch is missed, you have prevented the foot strike, and are probably still able to catch the knee or other part of the leg and will be able to get a countering rear-throw. It might require you to step towards your opponent with your left foot to get the throw if the grip is higher on his leg.

TECHNIQUES FROM A MUTUAL GRIP AT THE ARMS

Grabbing foot

Push away

finish

COUNTER TO THE GRIP AT THE BODY

It is important to know how to get away from a grip at the body if you choose not to wrestle at that distance.

> **This is a Wrestling at the Body**
>
> **When you grapple with an opponent so that you have one hand under his arm and the other above, and he has you also thus, and he is strong and presses you to him, then plant the elbow of the hand that you have above on his throat, and press him hard with it. Thus he must release you.**

TECHNIQUE (vD 103v.1)

1. Your opponent has you at the body grip with one arm over and one arm under, and he is strong and is squeezing you.

2. Take the elbow of your uppermost arm (Left shown) and drive it into his throat, pushing him back and to the right.

3. This will make him release his grip .

KEY POINTS

❖ He may have his face close to your body which will mean you need to start by slipping your hand between you and pushing forwards along your forearm to the elbow. This is fine, as long as you get your elbow in there to push with.

❖ Do not attempt to push him away with the "weak" of your arm, at the wrist. This will be ineffective against a very strong opponent.

Grip at the body

Counter

Grip at the body

THE WINNING STEP

This is a throw at the body which is similar to the break of the grip, but uses the press on the neck to throw him to the ground over a leg. I show this technique on the opposite side than is written, so as to maintain continuity with all of the rest of the throws.

Another Wrestling Technique

If your left arm is below, then fall with your right hand to his throat and step with your left foot behind his right and press him over it. Item: you can throw him off his feet on both sides.

TECHNIQUE (vD 106v.2)

1. Your opponent has you at the body grip with one arm over and one arm under.

2. Drive your right hand upwards and backwards into his throat, the pressure going under his jaw. Step with your right foot behind his left foot as you make the strike.

3. Press him over your leg to your right.

Driving right hand across neck

Pressing over leg

KEY POINTS

❖ When you go to press him at the neck, your thumb and first finger may end up underneath the jawbone giving a place of purchase for your hand.

❖ This pressure on the neck and jawbone will create enough pain to encourage him to move in the direction you want him to go.

VARIATIONS

❖ A similar throw is shown in Fabian von Auerswald, "The Winning Step" plates 23, 24.

Grip at the body

NECK KNEE REAR THROW – AT THE BODY

This technique is related to the Shoulder Knee Rear Throw discussed before, but this time done from a closer distance. When working at the body, the upper arm goes across the neck rather than across the chest. This allows us to control the opponent's body more effectively through pain and pushing his head back.

Another Wrestling at the Body

When you grapple with an opponent so that you have one hand below and the other above, and he has you thus also, then send the arm that is above under his chin to his neck, and push him hard away from you. And with the hand that is below, grasp his leg at the crook of the knee and pull with it toward you; thus he will be thrown.

TECHNIQUE (vD 103v.3)

1. Your opponent has you at the body grip with one arm over and one arm under.

2. Take your left hand and insert it on his neck underneath his chin with the pinky upwards

3. Press him away and to your left with a step forwards with your left foot

4. Grasp his right leg at the knee and lift hard, throwing him on his back before you.

Driving left hand across neck

Pressing over

KEY POINTS

❖ When you grasp his neck with your hand, you can hook your pinky underneath his jawbone, giving you purchase on his head.

❖ When you press him backwards, do so by opening your body rather than using just the strength of your arm.

Driving hand across neck

ELBOW TO THE BALANCE - AT THE BODY

This appears in the Wrestling at the Body techniques as a counter to the Neck-Knee Rear Throw. Ott's short line of explanation tells us that one can use the Elbow to the Balance in this fashion. I have elaborated how to perform this throw at the body for clarity's sake. The remainder of this passage is shown in the following technique, Elbow Strike Rear Throw – At the Body.

Item: if he wants to counter that technique and unbalance you by your elbow...

TECHNIQUE (vD 104r.1)

1. Your opponent has you at the body grip with one arm over and one arm under and he reaches across your neck to throw you backwards.

2. Grasp the outside of his left hand with your left hand. This is done best if you can grab his pinky and ring finger along with some meat of the hand.

3. Pull his hand away from your neck and lift it outwards, then downwards and and to your left side. This should create a wrist lock and point his elbow upwards, as well as to break his balance to his front balance point.

4. With your right hand, drive his elbow to your left side.

Grasp hand

Throw

KEY POINTS

❖ This technique is done the same as when it's shown at the arms, simply from a different distance.

❖ This use of the throw as a counter to their left arm coming across your body is related to when it is shown as a counter to the Same-Side Rear Throw.

Grasp hand

ELBOW-STRIKE REAR THROW - AT THE BODY

This throw is shown here as the counter to the Elbow to the Balance, as it is at the Arm Grip distance, above.

> **Item: if he wants to counter that technique and unbalance you by your elbow, then drop that same elbow and press it into his side. And with the other hand grasp his leg at the crook of the knee and throw him.**

TECHNIQUE (vD 104R.1)

1. Your opponent grabs your left hand with his left and intends to unbalance you with his right hand on your elbow and no longer has his right arm around your body.

2. Strike his right side with your left elbow, sinking down low and springing in with the left foot to power the strike and to get it behind his right foot.

3. Grab his right knee with your right hand, and lift it up to your chest.

4. At the same time, drive your left hand across his chest and throw him before you.

Strike the right side

Grasp the leg and pull

KEY POINTS

❖ This technique is the same as when it's done at the arms but is at a slightly closer distance.

Grip at the body

SHOULDER LOCK FORWARD THROW

This is a common throw in the German wrestling works and is useful when done at the arm distance, however Ott teaches it here at the body where it is easily executed.

Another Wrestling at the Body

When you grapple with an opponent so that you have one hand below and the other above, then send the arm that is below up from below outside above over the arm that he has above. And come to help with the other hand (the one you have above) and turn yourself away from him; thus he will fall. And that is good.

TECHNIQUE (vD 104r.3)

1. Your opponent has you at the body grip with one arm over and one arm under.

2. Drive your right arm over his left shoulder and grasp your own right wrist with your left hand securing the shoulder lock.

3. Step backwards with your left foot to throw him forwards.

Shoulder lock

Step back and drive down

finish

KEY POINTS

❖ This technique creates a strong shoulder lock that would be debilitating if maintained through an entire throw. Do not complete this throw in practice without releasing the lock.

❖ When you drive your arm over his shoulder, come over with your palm oriented to your face. This makes for a stronger lock than if your palm faces away.

VARIATIONS

❖ A similar throw is shown in Fabian von Auerswald, "The Hips and Elbows" plate 28.

Grip at the body

OPENING THROW

This throw tends to turn around the person being thrown, like opening a door. It can be tricky to do but if his legs are reversed to yours or if he has stepped between your legs this could be an effective counter and throw.

Another Wrestling at the Body

If you grapple with an opponent as described before, and he holds you loosely, then change the hand that you have below to his other side outside to the crook of his knee and lift with it. And with the hand that is above, go before his neck and push away from you above; thus he will fall.

TECHNIQUE (vD 104r.2)

1. Your opponent has you at the body grip with one arm over and one arm under and he holds you loosely.

2. With a deep step forwards with your left leg, drive your right arm around underneath to the outside of his right knee and lift it.

3. Drive your left hand in the front of his neck with the pinky upwards and push away and to your left.

Grasp knee

*Perspective shift
to the other side
for clarity*

KEY POINTS

❖ This technique can only work against someone who doesn't grip you strongly at the body.

❖ This may be a way to deal with an opponent whose legs are reversed to yours, his right leg forwards in this instance.

Lift and put hand on front of neck

LIFTING THROW

This technique is great for seizing the *Vor* in a grip at the body, entering from a grip at the arms. however, it would be very difficult for a smaller person to execute.

Another Wrestling Technique

Go through with your right hand, and grasp above the hip at his waist. And send your left hand above over his right shoulder, and grasp your right hand at the wrist and hold it fast and lift him up. And lift his left knee with your right knee, and throw him before you.

TECHNIQUE (vD 106R.2)

1. Begin by gaining the grip at the body, but maintain your initiative.

2. Step with your right knee to the outside of his left knee and throw him to your right side.

KEY POINTS

❖ This technique works best when you are bigger than your opponent and can rush in and maintain the pressure.

TECHNIQUES FROM A MUTUAL GRIP AT THE BODY

Grip at the body

Throw

Grip at the body below the arms

TURN-AROUND BACK BREAK

In this throw, as in the previous one, it is quite important that you be bigger than your opponent to be able to easily perform this maneuver since, again, you are basically lifting and throwing him. This is also the only technique in Ott's manuscript that describes a technique going "to the ground".

Another Wrestling Technique

When you have gone through his arms with both arms and he is small enough that you can well lift him, then do this: grasp him about the middle and clasp your hands together. And lift him to your left side and turn yourself around with him. And when you have turned around with him, then push him down to his knees and break his back toward you.

TECHNIQUE (vD 106v.3)

1. When you are significantly stronger than he is and can easily lift him.

2. Go below both of his arms with yours and clasp them behind his back.

3. Lift him and with your right leg forwards, throw him to the left so that your leg turns him around.

4. He will fall so that he lands on his knees, so turn and fall with your knees into his back and grasp underneath his chin to break his back towards you.

Lifting and throwing

KEY POINTS

❖ This technique really only works if you have a significant strength advantage on your opponent, but it does work really well in that instance.

❖ You will need to be prepared to follow him quickly to the ground if you wish to work from there.

Back Break

COUNTER TO THE TURN-AROUND BACK BREAK

This counter is identical to the Counter to the Grip at the Body with the interesting addition of being sure that your left foot is to the rear. This allows you to maximize your weight in the opposite direction that your opponent wants to throw you.

Counter This Thus

When he presses you to himself, then plant your elbow on his throat or chest and press him quickly from you, and so that your left foot is to the rear.

TECHNIQUE (vD 106v.4)

1. Your opponent grips you below your arms and is pressing you to himself.

2. Plant the elbow of your left arm into his neck and step backwards with your left leg

KEY POINTS

❖ Let your weight sink into your left leg when you do this so that you are maximizing the weight in the opposite direction to where he wants to throw you.

VARIATIONS

❖ You can also plant your elbow into his chest and push him back quickly.

TECHNIQUES FROM A MUTUAL GRIP AT THE BODY

Grip at the body below the arms

Press the neck and remove the leg

Collar grip

BREAKING A COLLAR GRIP

Whenever an opponent has a grip on your collar it is important to break his grip as quikly as possible to avoid being choked or throttled by him. While chokes aren't specifically dealt with in Ott's treatise, it is a threat that should not be ignored. Ott gives us escapes and techniques to handle this grip.

> **Item: if he grasps you in front by the collar with one hand and holds you fast, then turn your head through under his arm. Then he must release you. Or if you can grasp his thumb,[35] that is also good.**

TECHNIQUE (vD 107r.3)

1. Your opponent has gripped you in front by the collar with one hand.

2. Dip your head, driving your head through under his arm, then back up on the other side of his arm, which will make him release you. Be sure to bring your hands up to cover your face as you do this.

3. -OR- Grasp his thumb over the top with your hand and open it to that same side.

---

[35] This sub-technique is different from Ringeck's version.

Driving head under to break free

Grasp thumb over top

finish

*Perspective shifts
to the other side
for clarity*

KEY POINTS

❖ Paulus Kal (*In Service of the Duke,*
page 186) illustrates turning the
head through with both of his
hands up high protecting his face
as he comes through.

VARIATIONS

> **Item: if he grasps
> your collar from
> behind, then turn
> your head against
> him and through
> under his arm;
> thus you will get
> free.**

❖ Turning the head through also
works against a collar grip from
behind. (vD 107r.4)

❖ Paulus Kal (*In Service of the Duke,*
page 187) and Talhoffer 1443
(Plate 22) illustrate the thumb
grip combined with a knee kick or
shin rake. Ott himself makes no
mention of the kick in conjunction with breaking the grip.

Grip at the body, below the arms

BREAKING A GRIP FROM THE FRONT, UNDER THE ARMS

This series of techniques deals with breaking from a bear-hug style grip below. The assumption here is that the opponent is stronger than yourself and is going to dominate the encounter with this stregth. Ott advocates the use of a number of painful techniques to force a release.

Another Counter

Note: when an opponent has seized you under the arms and presses you hard to him, then break from him thus: grasp with both thumbs into his eyes or under his chin or to his throat; thus he must release you.

Another Wrestling Technique

When you are below with your arms, then you can grasp above to his throat or by the chin and break his neck over

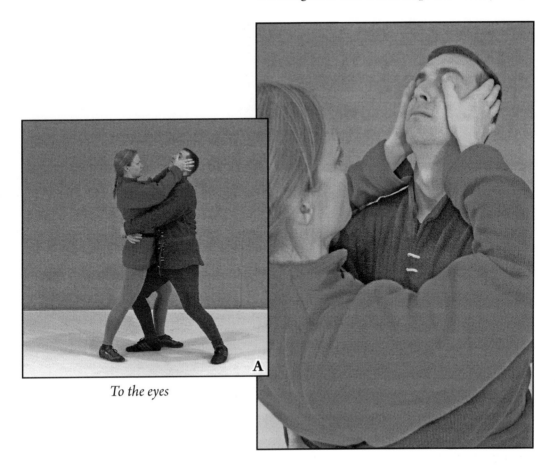

To the eyes

backward. Or you must go well through his arms with your arms.

Another Wrestling Technique

When he sends both his arms under both your arms, then go down from above with your arms outside and under his elbows, and close your arms together under his elbows, and lift upwards with strength and break his arms. You can also fall upon his throat when he has his arms underneath and press him backwards.

TECHNIQUE (vD 103v.2, vD 106v.1, vD 106r.4)

Your opponent has seized you around the body underneath both of your arms

A. Grasp his head and drive both thumbs into his eyes

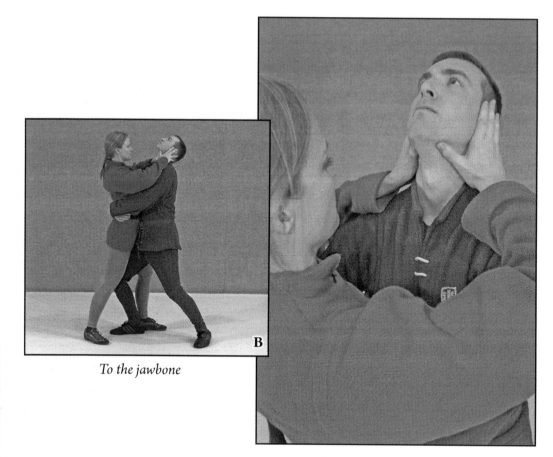

To the jawbone

BREAKING A GRIP FROM THE FRONT, UNDER THE ARMS (CONTINUED)

- OR -

B. Grasp his head and drive both thumbs under his jawbone and drive his head back

- OR -

C. Grasp his head and drive both thumbs into his throat

- OR -

D. Drive both arms outside his arms and under his elbows and close your arms together. Lift upwards hard and break his arms.

KEY POINTS

❖ These techniques work based on applying pain to your opponent. Use caution when practicing them.

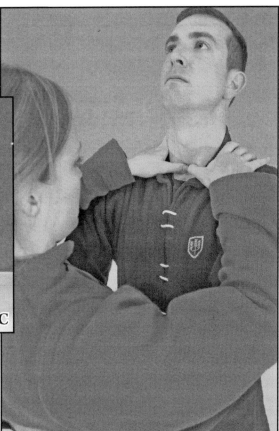

To the throat

Break the arms

Grip

Grasp the upper arm

BREAKING A GRIP FROM BEHIND, OVER THE ARMS: KNEE STOMP

This is a particularly vicious escape from a bear hug from behind over the arms. In it you grab your opponent's throat and step into his knee. This knee manipulation is unclear if you are simply collapsing it as you can do in a friendly match, or stepping on it so that it breaks. Both possibilities will allow you to continue the neck push and take even a bigger man to the ground.

Another Wrestling Technique

If someone grasps you from behind over the shoulders, then send your right arm over to the crook of his elbow on the side where the foot is forward. And come with the other hand to help press to the side straight from the outside. And hold his arm with the one hand and grasp his throat with the other. And step into the crook of the knee of his outward leg blocked toward you with the heel of your foot.

TECHNIQUE (vD 104v.1)

1. Your opponent has seized you around the body from behind over both of your arms.

2. Grasp his right elbow with your right hand and bring your left to grasp his right forearm.

Pull down and across

Stomp the knee

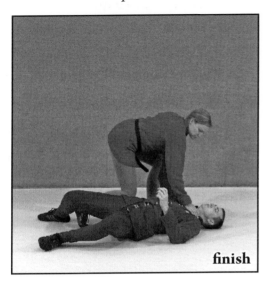

finish

3. Pull down and to the left, pulling him around your body

4. Hold his arm tightly with your left hand, send your right hand under between his arm and your body and drive to his throat

5. Step into his right knee with your right foot, either collapsing it or breaking it.

KEY POINTS

❖ The instructions for this technique assume his right foot is forward. If his left foot is forward, reverse all directions and do from the other side.

❖ This technique can break the knee, use caution when applying to your partner.

❖ You must pull his forearm with both hands, this is what will pull him forwards and create an opening so that you can strike to his throat.

VARIATIONS

• This technique also may be trying to describe an escape with a hip block. In that case, the right hand may be pulling his right elbow down and away to the right, while turning the body counter-clockwise inside the grip and blocking with the left hand against his right hip to continue the escape. From there you can continue as above, blocking against the throat and stomping into the knee.

Grip

BREAKING A GRIP FROM BEHIND, OVER THE ARMS: FORWARD THROW

This break of a grip is a great possibility for if the opponent is taller than yourself. You can quickly bend forwards and use his own grip against him, throwing him over your head.

Another Wrestling Technique

Item: if he grasps you from behind when you have your back turned to him, and he has seized you in his arms and above over his arms, then bend nimbly forward and throw him over your head.

TECHNIQUE (vD 107r.1)

1. Your opponent has seized you around the body over both of your arms from behind

2. Grasp both of his arms at the biceps with both of your hands.

3. Sink your weight low, bending at the knees.

4. Bend forwards quickly while straightening your knees to throw him forwards.

Grasp the arms

KEY POINTS

❖ You must move quickly for this to work or your opponent will sink his own weight and you will not be able to throw him forwards.

❖ This will not work if your opponent is significantly shorter than you.

Throw

Grip

BREAKING A GRIP FROM BEHIND, OVER THE ARMS: LEG BREAK

This break of a grip from behind will work well irregardless of the size of your opponent, as it relies upon attacking a lower opening. This is continued from the previous technique, but required a bit more explanation and so is given its own technique here.

… Or seize him below by one of his legs with one hand.

TECHNIQUE (vD 107r.1)

1. Your opponent has seized you around the body over both of your arms from behind.

2. Sink your weight low, bending at the knees.

3. If you feel that his leg is between your legs, grasp below his knee with one hand and yank upwards.

Sink, grab leg

KEY POINTS

❖ This technique is surprisingly effective if you drop your entire weight upon your partner's leg. Use caution when performing this technique in practice.

VARIATIONS

❖ Paulus Kal (*In Service of the Duke,* Tobler, Page 196) shows this technique done with two hands on the opponent's leg rather than one.

❖ If his leg is outside yours you can grasp it with the same-side arm and lift to throw him to that side.

Grip

BREAKING A GRIP FROM BEHIND, UNDER THE ARMS

This technique is common across many different martial arts styles.

Another Wrestling Technique

Item: if he has grasped you again from behind, and has his arms under your arms and has his hands open, then grasp him by a finger; thus he must let you go.

TECHNIQUE (vD 107r.2)

1. Your opponent has seized you around the body underneath both of your arms from behind and his hands are open.

2. Grasp one finger and rip it open to the side.

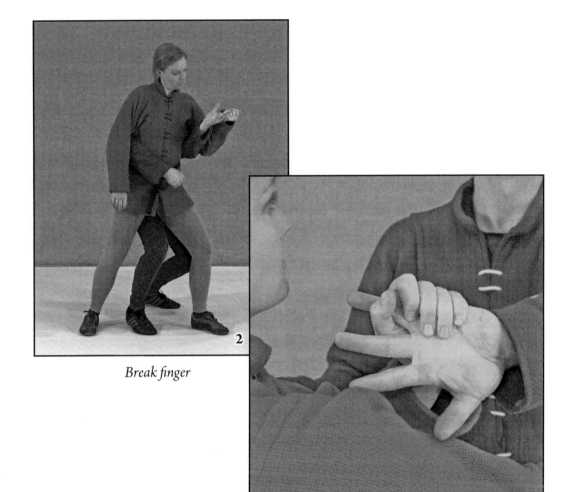

Break finger

Although from a different technique, this closeup shows the grip on the fingers.

KEY POINTS

❖ This will work using whichever finger you manage to hold and pull to a side.

❖ You can easily break a finger using this technique, so use caution when practicing.

Grip

BREAKING A GRIP FROM BEHIND, AT THE BELT

This technique involves breaking his balance through his grip upon your belt. It can work quite well and be very surprising to the person it is performed on, presuming it is executed with speed and dexterity.

Another Wrestling Technique

If he grasps you from behind by the belt, then sink down; and when he tries to lift you, then turn yourself around under him, and throw him over crosswise.

TECHNIQUE (vD 106r.1)

1. Your opponent has seized you from behind by the belt.

2. Sink your weight low, bending at the knees.

3. When you feel him try to lift you, turn around to your right and grasp him by the arms or neck.

4. Throw him over your right hip.

Sink and grab

Throw over hip

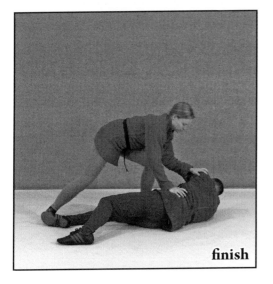

finish

KEY POINTS

❖ If you attempt this technique without the proper timing, he will simply pick you up by the belt. Be sure to sink your weight until you feel him strain against your weight, then quickly turn to get your grip.

❖ You must move quickly for this to work or your opponent will sink his own weight and you will not be able to throw him forwards.

Appendix A

FECHTBUCH 36

FOLIOS 100v – 107v

<VD100>   Here begins the wrestling composed by Master Ott, God have mercy on him, who was wrestler to the noble Princes of Austria.

In all wrestling should there be three things. The first is skill. The second is quickness. The third is the proper application of strength. Concerning this, you should know that the best is quickness, because it prevents him from countering you. Thereafter you should remember that you should wrestle a weaker man in the Before [*Vor*], an equal opponent simultaneously, and a stronger man in the After [*Nach*]. In all wrestling in the Before, attend to quickness; in all simultaneous wrestling, attend to the balance [*Waage*]; and in all wrestling in the After, attend to the crook of the knee.

<VD100v.1> **This is a Lesson**

When you want to wrestle with an opponent by the arms, then be mindful always to grasp him with your left hand by his right bicep, and with your right hand grasp him outside his left arm. And with your left hand that you have on his bicep, press sharply backwards, and with the right hand grasp his left hand in front and pull it hard to you. And when you have seized him thus, then use whichever of the following described wrestling techniques you think best.

<VD101r.1> **The First**

When you have grasped him with your left hand at his right bicep and with the right hand in front by his left hand, then send your left hand out from his right arm, and grasp him below his right elbow and pull it to you. And with your right hand, with which you have his left hand, push his arm from you; thus you wrench his arm.

<VD101r.2> **Another**

Item: when you have seized him as before, then lift his left arm with your right hand, and send your head through the arm and pull it over your neck. And with your left hand grasp his left leg at the crook of his knee, and throw him thus over your back.

<VD101r.3> **Another Wrestling from the First Hold**

Item: lift his left arm with your right hand and grasp him with your left hand under to his elbow and pull it to you. And with your right hand, push his arm away from you above, and spring with your left foot behind his right to throw him off his feet over your left leg.

<VD101v.1>[36] **Another Wrestling from the First Hold**

Item: hold his right hand fast with your left hand and grasp with your left hand to help your right. And hold his arm fast with both hands, and turn yourself through his arm to his right side; thus you overwhelm him from behind; or turn yourself through to your left side.

---

[36] There is indecipherable scrawling in the margin at the base of 101v.

<VD101v.2> **ANOTHER**

Item: hold his left hand fast with both hands and turn yourself through his arm to his left side, and pull his left arm over your right shoulder and break downwards.

<VD101v.3> **COUNTER THE TURNING THROUGH THUS:**

Item: when an opponent goes through you, then also go through, and fall to whichever of these wrestling techniques you wish.

VD101v.41> **NOTE THAT THIS TECHNIQUE COUNTERS ALL THE WRESTLING FROM THE FIRST STANCE** <VD101v.4>

Item: this is for when he has grasped your left hand with his right and intends to grasp through below onto your elbow with his left hand, intending to wrench your arm or to come to help his right hand and turn himself through your arm. Then note when he grasps with the left to help the right or grasps for your elbow, and simultaneously send your right arm over his left at his right side, seizing him by the waist. Spring with your right foot behind his left, and throw <102r> him off his feet over your right leg.

<VD102r.1> **ANOTHER WRESTLING TECHNIQUE**

Item: if he grasps your arms above with strength, and holds you fast and wants to press you, then send your right arm outside over his left in front by his hand, and grasp your right hand with your left hand. And press his hand with both of your hands toward your chest.

<VD102R.2> **NOTE:**

If he has his hand at your chest, then spring with your right foot behind his left, and grasp with your left hand to the crook of his left knee. And lift with that, and with your right hand push him above away from you; thus he will fall.

<VD102r.3> **ANOTHER NOTE:**

when you are pressing his hand in front to your chest with both of your hands, and he has his hand open and extends his fingers, then grasp him by the fingers with your left hand and lift upwards to your left side. And with your right hand, take him off balance by the elbow.

<VD102r.4> **ANOTHER WRESTLING TECHNIQUE**

When you want to wrestle with an opponent and he holds you loosely at the arms, then grasp with your left hand above over his right, and grasp his left hand by <102v> the fingers or otherwise, and lift towards your left. And with your right hand take him off balance by his elbow.

<VD102v.1> **COUNTER THAT THUS**

When someone does this, and grasps with his left hand to your fingers and wants to unbalance you with the right, then send your right hand under his left arm around the body. And spring with your right foot before both of his feet, and throw him thus over your right hip.

<VD102v.2> **OR COUNTER IT THUS**

When he has grasped your left hand with his left hand and wants to unbalance you with his right hand, then sink down, and go to him with your left elbow to his waist. Spring with your left foot behind his right foot, grasp his right leg with your right hand at the crook of his knee, and pull toward you. With the left push him away from you above; thus he will fall.

<VD102v.3> **ANOTHER**

Note: when he grasps your left hand with his left hand, and tries to unbalance you with his right and pushes your left elbow up in the air, then turn your head through and send your right arm to his left flank; and spring with your <103r> right foot behind his right foot, and throw him over your right hip. Or grasp one of his legs with your right hand as you turn through, and jerk him toward you.

<VD103r.1> **ANOTHER WRESTLING TECHNIQUE**

Item: when you have each grasped each other by the arms and he holds you loosely, then strike out his left arm down from above with your right hand. And grasp him with it in the crook of his left knee, and pull toward you and push in front on the left side of his chest with your left hand. Thus he must fall.

<VD103r.2> **COUNTER THAT THUS**

Note: when he grasps to your chest in front with his left hand, then grasp his left hand with your left, and take him off balance by his elbow with your right hand. Or push his elbow out with your right hand, straight upwards, and thus turn him away from you.

<VD103r.3> **ANOTHER WRESTLING TECHNIQUE**

When you each have each other by the arms and he holds you loosely, then strike his right hand out with your left hand downwards from above, and send it through below his right arm <103v> and grasp him behind. And hold him fast and pull towards you, and with your right hand grasp him outside to the crook of his right knee. Thus you throw him to the left side. This works on both sides.

<VD103v.1> **THIS IS A WRESTLING AT THE BODY**

When you grapple with an opponent so that you have one hand under his arm and the other above, and he has you also thus, and he is strong and presses you to him, then plant the elbow of the hand that you have above on his throat, and press him hard with it. Thus he must release you.

<VD103v.2> **ANOTHER COUNTER**

Note: when an opponent has seized you under the arms and presses you hard to him, then break from him thus: grasp with both thumbs into his eyes or under his chin or to his throat; thus he must release you.

<VD103v.3> **ANOTHER WRESTLING AT THE BODY**

When you grapple with an opponent so that you have one hand below and the other above, and he has you thus also, then send the arm that is above under his chin to his neck, and push him hard away from you. And with the hand that is below, grasp his leg at the crook of the knee and <104r> pull with it toward you; thus he will be thrown.

<VD104r.1> **ITEM:**

If he wants to counter that technique and unbalance you by your elbow, then drop that same elbow and press it into his side. And with the other hand grasp his leg at the crook of the knee and throw him.

<VD104r.2> **ANOTHER WRESTLING AT THE BODY**

If you grapple with an opponent as described before, and he holds you loosely, then change the hand that you have below to his other side outside to the crook of his knee and lift with it. And with the hand that is above, go before his neck and push away from you above; thus he will fall.

<VD104r.3> **ANOTHER WRESTLING AT THE BODY**

When you grapple with an opponent so that you have one hand below and the other above, then send the arm that is below up from below outside above over the arm that he has above. And come to help with the other hand (the one you have above) and turn yourself away from him; thus he will fall. And that is good.

<VD104r.4> **A COUNTER TO THE BAR** [37]

Note: when you each have grasped each other by the arms and you have <104v> your left foot forward, and he is then cunning and steps with his right foot outside behind your left and wants to jerk you over it by the arms, then quickly pull your left foot back. And with this, seize his right foot and push him above at the chest; thus he will fall.

---

[37] From this technique onward, the material tracks with the wrestling presented in the Ringeck manuscript as "Other Good Wrestling Techniques and Counters" (78r ff.)

<VD104v.1>   **ANOTHER WRESTLING TECHNIQUE**

If someone grasps you from behind over the shoulders, then send your right arm over to the crook of his elbow on the side where the foot is forward. And come with the other hand to help press to the side straight from the outside. And hold his arm with the one hand and grasp his throat with the other. And step into the crook of the knee of his outward leg blocked toward you with the heel of your foot.

<VD104v.2>   **ANOTHER WRESTLING TECHNIQUE**

Strike out his left hand with your right hand, and grasp the fingers of his right hand. Grasp his right arm which you struck upwards in front with your left hand, and throw him backwards over your left leg.

<VD104v.3>   **ANOTHER WRESTLING TECHNIQUE**

Strike out his left with your right hand, and send your right <105r> in front between his legs, seizing him behind by the doublet or on the arm. And lift him thus and push him away from you above with your left hand; thus he will fall backwards onto his head.

<VD105v.1>   **COUNTER THIS THUS**

When he sends his right hand through between your legs and seizes you behind by the doublet, then bend your head against him, and send both your arms through from the outside below his right arm, and lift upwards with it. Thus he cannot throw you.

<VD105v.2>   **ANOTHER WRESTLING TECHNIQUE**

If he grasps your left hand with both hands and wants to pull you to his right side, then send your right hand through from above over his left arm. And with this, send your right hand to grasp his right side, and with your left, fall to the crook of one of his knees.

<VD105v.3>   **ANOTHER WRESTLING TECHNIQUE**

If he seizes you in front by the chest with both hands, then send your right hand above over his left and control it, and send your left hand onto his right elbow. And create a barrier with your <105v> left foot.[38]

---

[38] The Ringeck manuscript advises to use the right foot, which seems less practical.

<*VD105v.1*>   **A Counter to a Bar**

When he tries to use a bar with his right hand, then bar with your left.

<*VD105v.2*>   **Another Wrestling Technique**

Strike out with both hands and fall to the crooks of both of his knees and pull them to you. And push him above with your head to his chest; thus he will fall.

<*VD105r.3*>   **Counter This Thus**

Grasp him above by the neck under his armpits, and place yourself right on him above. And step well back with your feet, so that he cannot grasp either one; thus you press him to the ground.

<*VD105r.4*>   **Another Wrestling Technique**

If he has his right foot forward, then pull his right hand with your left, and strike him with the left foot down to his right ankle. And thus jerk him down. Or fall with the right hand to his throat as you strike out his foot, and push him over backward.

<*VD105r.5*>   **Another Wrestling Technique**

If he holds you loosely by the arms, then grasp with your left hand to his right, and grasp him by the fingers. And hold him fast and strike up with your right hand, and go through under his right arm, <106r> and grasp him by the flank, and with your left hand at the crook of his knee.

<*VD106r.1*>   **Another Wrestling Technique**

If he grasps you from behind by the belt, then sink down; and when he tries to lift you, then turn yourself around under him, and throw him over crosswise.

<*VD106r.2*>   **Another Wrestling Technique**

Go through with your right hand, and grasp above the hip at his waist. And send your left hand above over his right shoulder, and grasp your right hand at the wrist and hold it fast and lift him up. And lift his left knee[39] with your right knee, and throw him before you.

---

[39] In Ringeck, it is the right arm that is used, not the knee. This confusion clouds the technique considerably.

<VD106r.3> **ANOTHER WRESTLING TECHNIQUE**

Grasp his right[40] hand with both hands and jerk him to your right side. And step with your right foot behind his right foot, and send your right arm to his left side and throw him over your right hip.

<VD106r.4> **ANOTHER WRESTLING TECHNIQUE**

When he sends both his arms under both your arms, then go down from above with your arms outside and under his elbows, and close your arms together under his elbows, and lift upwards with strength and break his arms. You can also fall upon his throat when he has his arms underneath and press him backwards. <106v>

<VD106v.1> **ANOTHER WRESTLING TECHNIQUE**

When you are below[413] with your arms, then you can grasp above to his throat or by the chin and break his neck over backward. Or you must go well through his arms with your arms.

<VD106v.2> **ANOTHER WRESTLING TECHNIQUE**

If your left arm is below, then fall with your right hand to his throat and step with your left foot behind his right and press him over it. Item: you can throw him off his feet on both sides.

<VD106v.3> **ANOTHER WRESTLING TECHNIQUE**

When you have gone through his arms with both arms and he is small enough that you can well lift him, then do this: grasp him about the middle and clasp your hands together. And lift him to your left side and turn yourself around with him. And when you have turned around with him, then push him down to his knees and break his back toward you.

<VD106v.4> **COUNTER THIS THUS**

Your opponent presses you to himself, then plant your elbow on his throat or chest and press him quickly from you, and so that your left foot is to the rear.

---

[40] In Ringeck, the left hand is pulled, making for a very awkward and seemingly impractical technique.

[41] In Ringeck, it is when you are above with your arms.

<VD106v.5> **ANOTHER WRESTLING TECHNIQUE**

Item: when he intends to go through your arm with his head and throw you over his back, grasp him by the neck with the same arm and press him hard to you. <107r> And place your chest on him above, and push him down with your weight.

<VD107r.1> **ANOTHER WRESTLING TECHNIQUE**

Item: if he grasps you from behind when you have your back turned to him, and he has seized you in his arms and above over his arms, then bend nimbly forward and throw him over your head. Or seize him below by one of his legs with one hand.

<VD107r.2> **ANOTHER WRESTLING TECHNIQUE**

Item: if he has grasped you again from behind, and has his arms under your arms and has his hands open, then grasp him by a finger; thus he must let you go.

<VD107r.3> **ITEM:**

If he grasps you in front by the collar with one hand and holds you fast, then turn your head through under his arm. Then he must release you. Or if you can grasp his thumb,[42] that is also good.

<VD107r.4> **ITEM:**

If he grasps your collar from behind, then turn your head against him and through under his arm; thus you will get free.

<VD107r.5> **ITEM:**

If he holds you with both hands in front of your chest, then push his right elbow up, and turn yourself through and grasp him at the waist.

<VD107r.6> **ANOTHER WRESTLING TECHNIQUE**

When you have grasped his right bicep with your left hand and you press him backward with it, and he falls with his right arm from outside over your left hand, and presses your hand fast to his chest, then send the same <107v> elbow to his right side and sink down. And spring with your left foot behind his right, and grasp with your right hand to the crook of his knee, and throw him down before you.

---

[42] This sub-technique is different from Ringeck's version.

Appendix B

Ott's Treatise across Manuscripts

D r. Ranier Welle graciously gave permission for the reprinting of this table from his work , '... *und wisse das alle höbischeit kompt von deme ringen' Der Ringkampf als adelige Kunst im 15. Und 16. Jahrhundert.* This table shows a comprehensive comparison of Ott's techniques from across the manuscripts within which it is written. This allows the student to easily pursue further research into possible copy errors when there is not clarity between the Von Danzig and Ringeck manuscripts which were noted in the translation above.

I regret that it was beyond the scope of this project to pursue this line of research at this time.

COMPARISON OF TECHNIQUES (DER KONKORDANZAPPARAT)

Ms. Chart. A 558	Ms. Dresd. C487	Cod. 44 A 8	Cod. I. 6.4*3	Cod. P 5126	M. I. 29	Ms. Germ. Quart. 2020 HS 7	o. S. Wassmannsdorff HS 9	Cod. 10826	Cgm 3712
Talhoffer	Ringeck	Danzig	Lew	Kal	Speyer	Goliath	Anon	Mair	Wilhalm
1443	1438-1450	1452	about 1450	1450-1490	1491	1510-1520	1539	about 1542	1556
1	2	3*	4	5	6	7	9	10	11
-	---	1	1	1	1	1	1	1	1
1	---	2	2	2	2	2	2	2	2
2	---	3	3	3	3	3	3	3	3
3	---	4	4	4	4	8	4	4	4
4	---	5	5	5	5	4	5	5	5
7	---	6	8	7	8	5	8	8	8
5	---	7	6	6	6	6	6	6	6
6	---	-	7	-	7	-	7	7	7
8	---	8	9	8	12	7	9	9	9
9	---	9	10	9	13	-	10	10	10
11	---	10	12	11	15	-	12	12	12
10	---	11	11	10	14	-	11	11	11
12	---	12	13	12	16	9	13	13	13
13	---	13	14	13	17	10	14	14	14
14	---	14	15	14	18	11	15	15	15
15	---	15	16	15	19	12	16	16	16
---	---	16	---	---	---	13	---	---	---
16	---	17	17	16	9	14	17	17	17
17	---	18	18	17	10	15	18	18	18
18	---	19	19	18	11	16	19	19	19
19	---	20	20	19	20	17	20	20	20
20	---	---	21	---	21	---	END	21	21
21		22	22	20	22	18		22	22
22		22	23	21	23	19		23	23
23		23	24	22	24	20		24	---
24		24	25	23	25	21		25	24
25		25	26	24	26	22		26	25
26		26	---	25	27	23		---	---
27		---	---	26	28	---		---	---
28	1	27	---	27	29	24		---	---
29	2	28	---	28	30	---		43	9**
---	3	29	---	29	31	---		44	10**
30	4	30	---	30	32	25		47	12**
31	---	---	---	31	33	---		---	---
32	5	31	27	32	34	26		27	26
33	6	32	28	33	35	27		28	---

Ms. Chart. A 558	Ms. Dresd. C487	Cod. 44 A 8	Cod. I. 6.4*3	Cod. P 5126	M. I. 29	Ms. Germ. Quart. 2020 HS 7	o. S. Wassmannsdorff HS 9	Cod. 10826	Cgm 3712
Talhoffer	Ringeck	Danzig	Lew	Kal	Speyer	Goliath	Anon	Mair	Wilhalm
1443	1438-1450	1452	about 1450	1450-1490	1491	1510-1520	1539	about 1542	1556
34	7	33	29	34	36	28		29	27
35	8	34	30	35	37	29		30	28
36	9	35	31	36	38	30		31	29
37	10	36	32	37	39	31		32	30
38	11	37	33	38	40	32		33	31
39	12	38	34	39	41	33		34	32
40	13	39	35	40	42	34		35	33
41	14	40	36	41	43	35		36	34
42	15	41	37	42	44	36		37	---
---	16	42	38	43	45	37	1	38	35
43	17	43	39	44	46	38	2	39	36
---	18	44	40	45	47	39	-	40	37
---	19	45	41	46	48	40	3	41	38
44	20	46	42	47	49	41	4	42	39
---	21	47	End	48	50	42	5	END	END
45	22	48		---	51	43	6		
---	---	---		---	---	44	-		
46	23	49		49	52	45	7		
---	24	50		50	53	46	8		
---	25	51		51	54	47	9		
47	26	52		52	55	---	10		
---	27	53		53	56	48	11		
---	28	54		---	57	49***	12		
48	29	55		---	58	50	13		
49	30	56		54	59	51	14		
---	---	---		55	60	---	---		
50	---	---		56	61	---	---		
51	31	57		57	62	52	15		

*   Leithandschrift (Primary Manuscript)

**   Aus der zweiten Ringkampflehre der Handschrift (From the second lesson on wrestling in the manuscript)

***   Der hier vorgeschlagene Bruch ("abnemen") wird in den übrigen Handschriften nicht explizit genannt. Er entspricht jedoch hinsichtlich seiner Struktur den anderen vorgeschlagenen Möglichkeiten des Bruches und weicht nur in einem Detail geringfügig ab.

The counter-technique described here (*Abnehmen*) isn't explicitly named in the other manuscripts. It corresponds, however, as to its structure, and differs only slightly from the technique in detail.

Appendix C

DRILLS AND CLASS NOTES

There are a variety of ways that you can drill wrestling techniques based, largely, on your goals as a student or instructor. I have included a few drills for what I consider to be the main points of interest for a student of medieval wrestling, but it is by far not an exhaustive list of possibilities, nor of drills themselves.

- ❖ Learning a Technique

- ❖ Technique Drills (single techniques)

- ❖ Fühlen Drills (using 2 or 3 techniques based on a single grip)

- ❖ Concept Drills (using techniques to explore *Hauptstücke*)

- ❖ Entry or Exit Drills (Getting grip, getting out of grip)

- ❖ Sparring (Free-wrestling competitively)

Above all, use your creativity to find new ways to look at the "same old" material.

LEARNING A TECHNIQUE
NOTES:

❖ When learning a technique it is imperative that you give and receive the exact same setup with each repetition.

❖ Do NOT counter your partner's attempt to learn the technique. This only frustrates him and doesn't instruct either of you.

❖ Break the technique down into steps, and as each step becomes familiar, begin to blur the lines between each step until the throw is done as a single motion.

❖ Do not disregard the instructions on the setup.

SOLO DRILLS:

❖ You should practice each throw alone, imagining the position and power of the opponent. This will help solidify for you what your body should be doing regardless of the exact specifics of what his body is up to.

❖ Think of this as "shadow boxing" with wrestling techniques.

❖ This is a great way to train at home and anytime you lack a partner. It also helps you to see and correct the disparity between your imagined response and your actual response when a partner is there.

PAIRED DRILLS – STEP BY STEP, FITTING IN:

❖ Practice each throw with a partner, especially when first learning the throw, by breaking it down to each step and practicing it in order. Enter distance, achieve the proper position and break the opponent's balance but do not complete the throw.

❖ Learning a technique this way allows you to go slow enough to get the order correct on a throw, especially when it's important.

❖ Simply "fitting in" (achieving the final position where the throw occurs), rather than completing every throw, allows you to get a large number of practice throws. Falling is hard work, and taking fifty falls in a row can be damaging and exhausting for your partner.

PAIRED DRILLS – AT SPEED AND WITH SMOOTHNESS, FITTING IN:

❖ Practice each throw with a partner, once you understand all of the steps that should be included in a throw, by performing it at speed and as smoothly as you can.

❖ Again "fitting in", rather than completing every throw, allows you to get a large number of practice throws without being unnecessarily abusive to your partner.

❖ You should be looking to be sure that your body is in correct position each time and that you are effectively breaking your opponent's balance during each throw.

PAIRED DRILLS – AT SPEED AND WITH SMOOTHNESS, COMPLETING THE THROW:

❖ Practice each throw with a partner, once you understand all of the steps that should be included in a throw and can reliably break the opponent's balance, by performing it at speed and as smoothly as you can.

❖ Now once their balance is broken, follow through with a full throw. Do not train yourself to hold back at this point. You should treat each throw as if it is done perfectly and will work as written.

PAIRED DRILLS – GAINING STRENGTH IN THE THROW:

❖ This may take some imagination to use with different throws, but one wonderful drill that can be used to practice one's entry and breaking balance is to train against two partners working together, effectively doubling the weight against which one is working.

❖ You may also use resistance bands or martial arts belts to practice pulls and entries. Use your imagination!

TECHNIQUE DRILLS

This is an example of one way to explore a single technique (the Elbow-Strike Rear Throw in this example). By performing a single technique against a variety of grips and throws you see the unifying opening that is required to be able to use a given technique. This exploration is important once you have learned how to perform the throw in a basic sense. If, however, you are still not sure of how to perform the throw and need to be talked through it, this drill is not appropriate and you should go back to the drilling style in Learning a Technique.

PAIRED DRILL – LEARNING TO RESPOND TO GRIP CHANGES:

❖ Practice each throw with a partner, especially when first learning the throw, by breaking it down to each step and practicing it in order. Fit in for the throw, but do not complete. You can eventually travel the same training path outlined above, but now focusing on how that throw can be used from a variety of entries.

For instance, if Aron and I are in an equal grip, and he senses I am weak at the grip, he can break free and grab for my fingers. I will then want to counter that action by striking his ribs with my elbow. If I cannot respond *Indes* to his action, he will throw me with the Elbow to the Balance. If I can respond quickly enough in the moment, I will throw him with the Elbow-Strike Rear Throw.

The point of this drill is to respond to the changes in the grip and applying the appropriate throw. It helps train how to respond in the right time.

FÜHLEN DRILLS

This is an example of a drill to explore *Fühlen*, or "Feeling". In *Fighting with the German Longsword*, Christian Tobler describes *Fühlen* as:

"The skill of sensing the degree of pressure exerted by one's opponent in a bind. One should determine how to react to an opponent by sensing whether he is "hard" or "soft" at the sword."

This is a vital skill to a wrestler, the ability to sense the opponent's intention through the grip on his body and to react appropriately.

❖ Practice each throw with a partner, especially when first learning the throw, by breaking it down to each step and practicing it in order. Fit in for the throw, but do not complete. You can eventually travel the same training path outlined above, but now focusing on how the opponent's changing pressure requires me to change my countering throw.

❖ The previous drill trained applying a technique in the right time. This drill trains applying the throw in the right direction as well as the proper time.

In this example, Aron and I are working from the body. Aron will begin by entering and getting the grip at the body. If I respond quickly enough, I can counter that by using the Counter to the Grip at the Body. But if I miss that counter, then I have a couple of options, I can pull backwards, trying to get out of the grip, or I can push into him, hoping to effect the counter.

Aron will then respond to my pressure and either throw me to the rear if I pull backwards or throw me forwards if I push into him.

Concept Drills

In Liechtenauer's verse, he describes the *Hauptschtuke* or the "Chief Techniques" with the Longsword. Many of these techniques are not relevant only to fighting with the longsword, but rather are concepts that apply to the art as a whole. There are five special blows and twelve concepts, and while it's beyond the scope of this work to explore ways to apply them to the entire art, I feel it's important to give a single example so that the reader may be inspired to explore these further in his own studies.

Nachreisen is translated as "chasing" and is the concept of following his movements with an attack that goes in the same direction as he is moving.

A classic example of *Nachreisen* being used in Ott's treatise is if Aron and I are at an equal grip at the arms. He can attempt to throw me using Elbow to the Balance. But, as his left arm leaves my right arm to grasp my left hand, I follow his left arm with my right and throw him using the Forward Hip Throw.

For the student who is interested in studying medieval wrestling as a portion of the greater *Kunst des Fechten* it is important to begin to study these throws as examples of known fighting principles, not considering them as a separate art.

Entry and Exit Drills

There are not many places where Ott gives us explicit instruction on how to enter safely into a grip, but we do have some suggestions of the types of grips one might find oneself in and how to work from them. Therefore, it is of interest to us to explore ways to come into gripping distance, be it at the arms or the body.

We can practice entering against an opponent and gaining the grip we want, be it Ott's grip at the arms, grabbing one arm with both of ours, or entering to attack the body. One fun way to incorporate this practice is to have one student (Student A) stand ready to receive opponents. Student A's job is to prevent those entering from gaining their grip upon him. One opponent (Student B) will enter and attempt to get the grip of his choice. If Student A repels that grip, he will stay in the center to receive another opponent (Student C). If, however, Student B gains the grip he intended, he then stays to receive Student C and will now be attempting to repel Student C's attempts to gain a grip.

Sparring

Finally, we come to sparring, which is likely the point to which every student eventually wants to get. The difficulty in sparring using medieval wrestling techniques is that these techniques often rely upon joint locks or application of pain to break an opponent's balance. Because of this, I must urge caution and encourage each student to spend a large amount of time learning to fall correctly and gently, to learn to apply these throws with varying amounts of pressure to joints and to learn to roll with throws so that one releases pressure upon the joint in question rather than adding to the pressure. Study all of these techniques, and consider how some of them may be altered slightly to minimize the risk to shoulder joints. It can be simply done in most cases.

As you move forwards in your practice making each of these throws more and more vigorous, also learn to be a "good" opponent. That is, learn to take falls cleanly. Learn when it is safe to fight against a throw and when it will result in injury. Competition is good, and a competitive nature is what drives us to perform better in our study of martial arts. Competitiveness, however, has a dark side and can lead to pain, injury or death. Increase the power and amplitude of these throws with foresight and caution between yourself and an opponent who is ready for that level of power.

If you choose to add techniques from other masters to focus your wrestling practice on self-defense and combative uses, consider how that will change the game as a whole. I would encourage you to then invest in padded helmets and foot and hand protectors, and learn to enter and exit distance avoiding and blocking punches and kicks. This is good study, and one I would absolutely encourage for the student of the greater Art.

Because Ott does not deal with groundwork, punching or kicking, you can easily limit yourself to the techniques contained within this work, wrestle to the third fall, and have a wonderfully challenging match. Do not discount his work as "simply" sportive: the lessons contained within his work will serve you well, whatever your focus.

BIBLIOGRAPHY

PRIMARY SOURCES

Anonymous, *Fechtbuch* (c. 1430), Ms. KK 5013, Kunsthistorisches Museum, Vienna, Austria.

Anonymous, *Fechtbuch* (after 1400). Cod. I.6.4º.2, Universitätsbibliothek Augsburg, Augsburg, Germany.

Anonymous, *Fechtbuch* (15th c.), Cod. Guelf. 78.2 Aug. 20, Herzog August Bibliothek, Wolfenbüttel, Germany.

Anonymous, *Fechtbuch* (15th c.), Cod. Vindob. B 11093, Österreichische Nationalbibliothek, Vienna, Austria.

Anonymous, *Fechtbuch* (c. 1500), Cod. 862, Fürstl. Fürstenbergische Hofbibliothek, Donaueschingen, Germany

Anonymous, *Fechtbuch* (after 1500), Libr. Pict. A83, Staatsbibliothek Preußischer Kulturbesitz, Berlin, Germany.

Anonymous, *Gladiatoria* (1st half of 15th c.), MS. germ. quart. 16, Jagelonische Bibliothek, Krakau, Poland.

Anonymous, *Goliath* (1st quarter of 16th c.), MS. germ. quart. 2020, Jagelonische Bibliothek, Krakau, Poland.

Auerswald, Fabian von, *Ringer Kunst: fünff und achtzig stücke zu ehren Kurfürstlichen gnaden zu Sachsen etc.* VD 16 A 4051, Georg-August-Universität Göttingen, Göttingen, Germany.

Brakelond, Jocelin de fl. 1173-1215. *The chronicle of Jocelin of Brakelond, concerning the acts of Samson, abbot of the monastery of St. Edmund.* Translated from the Latin with introd., notes and appendices by H. E. Butler. (New York, Oxford University Press, 1949) and (London, New York, T. Nelson, [1951].)

Czynner, Hans, *Fechtbuch* (1538), Ms. 963, Universitätsbibliothek, Graz, Austria.

Döbringer, Hanko, *Fechtbuch* (1389), Codex Ms. 3227a, German National Museum, Nuremburg.

Danzig, Peter von, *Fechtbuch* (1452), Codex 44 A 8, Library of the National Academy, Rome, Italy.

Eyb, Ludwig von, *Kriegsbuch* (c. 1500), Ms. B 26, Universitätsbibliothek Erlangen, Germany.

Falkner, Peter, *Fechtbuch* (end of 15th c.), Ms. KK 5012, Kunsthistorisches Museum, Vienna, Austria.

Kal, Paulus, *Fechtbuch* (c. 1470), CGM 1507, Bayerische Staatsbibliothek, Munich, Germany.

Kal, Paulus, *Fechtbuch* (late 15th c. copy), Cod. S554, Zentralbibliothek, Solothurn, Switzerland

Kal, Paulus, *Fechtbuch* (late 15th c. copy), Ms. KK 5126, Kunsthistorisches Museum, Vienna, Austria.

Lecküchner, Johannes (1478), *Fechtbuch*, Cod. Pal. Germ. 430, Universitätsbibliothek Heidelberg, Germany

Lecküchner, Johannes (1482), *Fechtbuch*, Cgm. 582, Bayerische Staatsbibliothek, Munich, Germany.

(Jud) Lew, *Fechtbuch* (c. 1450), Cod.I.6.4°.3, Universitätsbibliothek Augsburg, Germany

Liberi da Premariacco, Fiore dei, *Il Fior Battaglia* (1409), MS Ludwig XV.13, Getty Museum, Los Angeles, USA.

Mair, Paulus Hector, *Fechtbuch* (1542), Mscr. Dresd. C93 / 94, Sächsische Landesbibliothek, Dresden, Germany.

Mair, Paulus Hector, *Fechtbuch* (1542), Cod. Vindob. 10825 / 26, Österreichische Nationalbibliothek, Vienna, Austria.

Meyer, Joachim, *Grundtliche beschreibung der freyen ritterlichen und adelichen kunst des fechtens* (A Thorough Description of the Free, Knightly and Noble Art of Fencing). Strasbourg, 1570

Ringeck, Sigmund, *Fechtbuch* (c.1440), Dresden, State Library of Saxony, Ms. Dresd. C 487.

Speyer, Hans von, *Fechtbuch* (1491), M I 29, Universitätsbibliothek Salzburg, Germany.

Sutor, Jakob, New Künstliches *Fechtbuch* (1612), Frankfurt am Main, Germany.

Talhoffer, Hans, *Fechtbuch*, (1443), Ms. Chart. A558, Forschungsbibliothek Gotha, Germany.

Talhoffer, Hans, *Fechtbuch*, (1450?), HS XIX, 17-3, Gräfl. Schloss Königseggwald, Germany.

Talhoffer, Hans, *Fechtbuch* (1459), Thott 290 2°, Königliche Bibliothek, Copenhagen, Denmark.

Talhoffer, Hans, *Fechtbuch* (1467), Cod. icon. 394a, Bayerische Staatsbibliothek, Munich, Germany.

Wilhalm, Jörg, *Fechtbuch* (1522/23), CGM 3711, Bayerische Staatsbibliothek, Munich, Germany.

Wilhalm, Jörg, *Fechtbuch* (1556), CGM 3712, Bayerische Staatsbibliothek, Munich, Germany.

SECONDARY SOURCES

Amberger, J. Christoph, *The Secret History of the Sword*. Baltimore, Maryland, Hammerterz Verlag, 1996.

Besant, Walter, *Medieval London: Historical and Social.* London, 1906

Carew, Richard, *Survey of Cornwall.* London, 1602.

Colón Semenza, Gregory M., Sports, *Politics, and literature in the English Renaissance.* Cranbury, New Jersey, Rosemont Publishing & Printing Corporation, 2003.

Colón Semenza, Gregory M., "Historicizing 'Wrastlynge' in the Miller's Tale," The Chaucer Review, volume 38, No. 1, Penn State University Press, 2003.

Diem, Carl, *Weltgeschichte des Sports und der Leibeserziehung, Cotta*; Auflage: Sonderausg, 1960.

Dunning, Eric & Malcolm, Dominic, "The Development of Sport," Sport: Critical Concepts in Sociology. New York, New York, Routledge, 2003.

Fleischer, Nat, *From Milo to Londos: The Story of Wrestling Through the Ages*, The Ring Athletic Library, 1936.

Gardiner, E. Norman, *Athletics of the Ancient World*, Oxford, 1930.

Hassall, W. O., "The Theater of Devotion: East Anglican Drama and Society in the Late Middle Ages" Modern Language Review 33.

Ledeboer, Suzanne, *A Basic Guide to Wrestling*, Griffin Publishing Group, 2001.

Mangan, J.A., *Sport in Europe: Politics, Class and Gender*, London, Frank Cass Publishing, 1999.

Marcus, Jacob Rader, *The Rise and Destiny of the German Jew.* Cincinnati, Union of American Hebrew Congregations, 1934.

Meyers, John C., *Wrestling: From antiquity to Date*, St. Louis, Selbstverlag, 1931.

Minkowski, Helmut, *Das Ringen im Grüblein: eine spätmittelalterliche Form des deutschen Leibringens*, Hoffmann, 1963.

Morton, Gerald W. and O'Brien, George M., *Wrestling to Rasslin': Ancient Sport to American Spectacle*, Bowling Green State University Popular Press, 1985.

Newman, Paul B., *Daily Life in the Middle Ages*, Jefferson, North Carolina, McFarland and Company, 2001.

St. Isidore (of Seville), *The Etymologies of Isidore of Seville.* Translated by Barney, Stephen A. et al. Cambridge, Cambridge University Press, 2006.

Ohlgren, Thomas H., *Medieval Outlaws: Twelve Tales in modern English Translation.* West Lafayette, Indiana, Parlor Press, 2005.

Poliakoff, Michael B., *Combat Sports in the Ancient World*, Yale University, 1987.

Talhoffer, Hans, *Medieval Combat: A Fifteenth-Century Illustrated Manual of Swordfighting and Close-Quarter Combat.* Edited Mark Rector, London, Greenhill Books, 2000.

Tobler, Christian Henry, *Fighting with the German Longsword.* Union City, California, Chivalry Bookshelf, 2004.

Tobler, Christian Henry, *In Saint George's Name.* Wheaton, Illinois, Freelance Academy Press, 2010.

Tobler, Christian Henry, *In Service of the Duke: The 15th Century Fighting Treatise of Paulus Kal.* Highland Village, Texas, Chivalry Bookshelf, 2006.

Tobler, Christian Henry, *Secrets of German Medieval Swordsmanship: Sigmund Ringeck's Commentaries on Johannes Liechtenauer's Verse.* Union City, California, Chivalry Bookshelf, 2001.

Wassmanndorf, Karl, et al, *Die Ringer-Kunst des Fabian von Auerswald.* M. G. Priber, 1869.

Welle, Rainer, *"... und wisse das alle hobischeit kompt von deme ringen": Der Ringkampf als adelige Kunst im 15. und 16. Jahrhundert Eine Sozialhistorische Und Bewegungsbiographische Interpretation Aufgrund Der Handschriftlichen Und Gedruckten Ringlehren Des Spatmittelalters*, 1993.

Wymer, Norman, *Sport in England: A History of Two Thousand Years of Games and Pastimes*, London, 1949.

Zabinski, Grzegorz with Bartlomiej Walczak, *Codex Wallerstein: A Medieval Fighting Book on the Longsword, Falchion, Dagger, and Wrestling.* Boulder, Colorado, Paladin Press, 2002.

PGIL2020USA